CRH provides a friendly and supportive pathway for those desiring to reconnect with their Catholic Faith — it is a journey of mercy and love.

*Mike Humphrys, Evangelisation Brisbane*
*Archdiocese of Brisbane*

I've been very blessed by starting Catholics Returning Home at St. Pius X in Lafayette, Louisiana. For over six years we have offered CRH twice a year and now three times per year, all the while witnessing a beautiful, spiritual transformation in those participating. Just recently I turned over the reins to a fellow facilitator, Phyllis Comeaux, who is very excited. Souls returning to God and the Church, what a joy witnessing the process. Also have been privileged to help other parishes start their CRH programs by hosting Sally Mews for a Diocese of Lafayette CRH Conference at St. Pius X.

Many Thanks to Sally Mews and the USCCB for presenting and approving CRH!

*Ashton J. Mouton Jr.*
*Minister of Evangelization, Lafayette, Louisiana*

Sally's Catholics Returning Home program is a must have in all of our parishes. Easy to implement and life changing for Catholics finding their way back to the Eucharist!

*Mike Browning*
*St. John Apostle & Evangelist Church*
*Mililani, Hawaii*

When I served at Holy Name Cathedral in Chicago, we used Catholics Returning Home as an instrument of reaching out to our brothers and sisters who had fallen away from the practice of the Catholic faith, and it was very fruitful. God bless Sally Mews for her contribution to the important work of the New Evangelization!

*Reverend Ronald T. Kunkel, S.T.D.*
*Assistant Professor, Department of Dogmatic Theology*
*Mundelein Seminary, Illinois*

Sally Mews began outreach to alienated Catholics many years ago, when no one was talking about it. She was an alienated Catholic herself and experienced what they were going through.

For many years, the Church has prayed to find a way to bring former Catholics back to living their faith. Parishes have sought to discover a program they might use to bring these Catholics back home.

It is my impression that parishes offering Catholics Returning Home as Sally describes in her newly revised book *Parish Guide for Implementing Catholics Returning Home* will bring many back to the Church.

*Bishop Roger W. Gries, O.S.B.*
*Auxiliary Bishop Emeritus of Cleveland, Ohio*

# Parish Guide for Implementing Catholics Returning Home Ministry

## Outreach to Non-Practicing Catholics

### Sally L. Mews

Leonine Publishers
Phoenix, Arizona

Cover image: "Jesus, the Good Shepherd" window, by Cadetgray, licensed under CC BY-SA 3.0 (https://commons.wikimedia.org/wiki/File:Jesus_the_good_Shepherd.jpg).

Scripture citations are from the Saint Joseph Edition of *The New American Bible*, copyright © 1970 by the Catholic Book Publishing Co., New York.

Published by

Leonine Publishers LLC
Phoenix, Arizona, USA

ISBN-13: 978-1-942190-45-5

Library of Congress Control Number: 2018951613

Printed in the United States of America

10 9 8 7 6 5 4 3 2 1

Visit us online at www.leoninepublishers.com
For more information: info@leoninepublishers.com

This book is dedicated to

the memory of the late Alvin Illig, C.S.P., founder of the
Paulist National Catholic Evangelization Association,
who affirmed, encouraged, and inspired me to follow
his leadership in ministry to non-practicing Catholics,

and to
my beloved husband, Harvey F. Mews, Jr.,
who is my best friend, advisor, lifelong
companion and partner in everything, including
ministry to non-practicing Catholics.

~

Sally L. Mews

# Table of Contents

# Acknowledgements

Many thanks to:

The late Fr. William McKee, C.Ss.R., pioneer and forerunner in ministry to inactive Catholics.

Msgr. Thomas Cahalane, Tucson, Arizona, founder of Alienated Catholics Anonymous.

Gerald F. Kicanas, Bishop Emeritus of Tucson, Arizona, former Auxiliary Bishop of the Archdiocese of Chicago, Illinois, for his continued encouragement and support.

Deacon John Rex, Archdiocese of Chicago, Illinois, Clergy Representative for Catholics Returning Home, for his support, guidance, and gifted graphic arts talent and skill in crafting the advertising and promotional materials for CRH. https://lighthouseprinting.net/catholics-returning-home/

Terrie Baldwin, Director of Evangelization, Diocese of Cleveland, for her steadfast support and years of CRH experience and insight.

James Louviere, Lafayette, Louisiana, Catholic filmmaker and TV producer, for his proofreading and theological guidance. http://www.gotruth.com

All the archdioceses, dioceses, parishes, and individuals who have shared their knowledge and experiences in order to enrich this ministry.

# Foreword

Sally Mews knows the pain of what it means to be away from the Church. She was once away herself. She has heard the stories of many who have left the Church and then reached out to return. Many of us, like Sally, may know of this pain. It may be from personal experience or through knowing the hurt or sadness of someone who is close to us. Accompanying others on this journey back to God's merciful arms is a ministry of love, healing, and reconciliation.

The Parable of the Lost Sheep is Sally's favorite analogy describing this healing and uplifting process, both in the reaching out and the finding. She was once the lost sheep and now she is reaching out and helping others through the program she created, Catholics Returning Home.

In this revised edition of her book *Inviting Catholics Home: A Parish Program*, Sally shares an updated "how-to" version of Catholics Returning Home, a "cheap, easy, and effective process" for parish communities to reach out to those missing from the pews. With the support of the pastor and a few team members, it can be done both easily and inexpensively. This quick-read book offers all you need to start it in any parish. The process is as simple as it sounds.

Over the past fifteen years, the Diocese of Cleveland has welcomed people back to the Faith, some having been gone up to 40 years before attending Catholics Returning Home. What a joy it has been to share in the many stories of those who have participated and experienced God's love and mercy in coming back to the Faith.

Sally Mew's wisdom comes from many years of developing, training, and experiencing successful Catholics Returning Home programs across the United States. Sally knows so well the ministry of healing and reconciliation. "Through the grace of the Lord working in their hearts," powerful transformations can and do occur through Catholics Returning Home.

Terrie Baldwin
Director of Evangelization
Diocese of Cleveland
September 2017

## Introduction

# From a Non-Practicing Catholic to an Evangelist — With God Anything Is Possible

My ministry to non-practicing Catholics was born out of my own anger and pain. I know firsthand what it feels like to be angry and to feel separated from the Church because I was in that position for many years. I never imagined in my wildest dreams that I would ever return to the Catholic Church, much less actually end up leading a ministry to help others come back!

I was born into a non-practicing Catholic family that was plagued by alcoholism, illness, and poverty. Except for a couple weeks of summer catechism, I had no contact with the Church. However, when I was in fourth grade, my family relocated due to my father's job. My parents decided to enroll me, my sister, and my brother in a Catholic school because it was located close to our home.

The setting was the pre-Vatican fifties, which meant black-and-white answers from the Baltimore Catechism.

Since I had limited contact with the Church prior to attending the school, I had no exposure to the Baltimore Catechism or the answers therein. I figured a "daily missal" had more to do with the space program and Sputnik than with the Catholic Church. As a result, I received a lot of negative attention from peers and teachers alike.

In addition, my family's poverty and dysfunction prevented them from paying full tuition for me and my siblings — a fact we were continuously reminded of. I vividly remember the shame and hopelessness of being held responsible for something at a young age over which I had no control.

I spent many years angry at the Catholic Church and searching for an alternative. I looked at other religions and at times considered myself a non-denominational Christian. Eventually I started reading the Bible, though I didn't read it end to end. Rather, I concentrated on the Psalms and the Gospels. Throughout this process, I felt a profound sense of conversion. I especially identified with the Gospel outcasts with whom Jesus was fraternizing.

I researched the origins of the Catholic Church and — after much prayer, discernment, and personal struggle — I realized I was a Catholic Christian. I also realized that the Catholic Church is made up of imperfect people who do make mistakes. So I returned to the Catholic Church. However, I did so quietly since it seemed that no one had noticed that I have been away or that I had returned.

When I returned to the Church, I didn't find the Church I had left. Instead, I found an incredible array of "ministries" and lay involvement. I had changed but so did the Church!

I felt a growing need to share the "good news" with other non-practicing Catholics. I felt called to reach out to those alienated, inactive Catholics — those people who felt as hurt and separated from the Church as I did when I was away for all those years. As a result, I embarked on a path which resulted in the design, testing, and implementation of a parish-based program I called "Catholics Returning Home (CRH)" to help non-practicing Catholics return to active practice of their faith. Since then, CRH has spread across the US and other countries and has become a classic because it's time tested and proven. I am hoping that this book *Parish Guide for Implementing Catholics Returning Home Ministry* will make it even easier for parishes everywhere to start this ministry to help bring our non-practicing brothers and sisters home to their Catholic faith.

## Chapter 1

# Jesus, the Good Shepherd, Is Our Model for Outreach to Non-Practicing Catholics

## Parable of Divine Mercy

The tax collectors and sinners were all gathered around to hear him, at which the Pharisees and the scribes murmured, "This man welcomes sinners and eats with them." Then he addressed this parable to them:

"Who among you, if he has a hundred sheep and loses one of them, does not leave the ninety-nine in the wasteland and follow the lost one until he finds it? And when he finds it, he puts it on his shoulders in jubilation. Once arrived home, he invites friends and neighbors in and says to them, 'Rejoice with me because I have found my lost sheep.' I tell you, there will likewise be more joy in heaven over one repentant sinner than over ninety-nine righteous people who have no need to repent" (Luke 15:1-10).

## Tending our lost sheep

We all know friends, family, and acquaintances who have drifted away from the Church. There are millions of them. And in any given parish, over half of the registered members don't regularly attend Mass. So, as disciples, what are we to do? Pray for them of course. Be an example for them as we live out our faith. But, we are also called to do more, and Jesus the Good Shepherd is our model for action. In the Parable of the Lost Sheep, Jesus the Good Shepherd left the ninety-nine to follow and search for the lost one until he found it. He brought it back to the fold where friends and neighbors rejoiced and celebrated with jubilation. Shouldn't we as disciples follow in Jesus' footsteps and reach out and seek those who have strayed and help them return? So many returnees say they didn't return earlier because no one ever asked them. So, our mission is to ask and ask, and ask yet again!

People leave the Church for many reasons. Relatively few people leave because of theological differences. Some leave because of boredom, indifference, ignorance, and misunderstanding of the basic beliefs of the Church. With the secularization of our society, more and more children are not raised with good Catholic role models in their own homes. Many Catholic parents put their kids in Catholic schools or their parish's religious education program (PSR) but are minimally knowledgeable or involved with their own Catholic faith. Is it any wonder that so many PSR and Catholic school kids drop out of their Catholic faith soon after their sacraments of initiation are completed? These people usually don't have any anger toward the Church. As they grow into adulthood, many want to return to the Church for Marriage, or Baptism for their children, at which time they re-engage with their Catholic faith.

Other people leave the Church because of anger and hurts — real or imagined — caused by representatives of the Church and/or they're mad at God. For these people, they have a real struggle with returning, until they wrestle with and work through their anger. Some people blame God for the death of loved ones. Why did God take my loved one away from me? For others, they may have been having difficulties or hard times with other areas of their life, and then the Church or a church representative did something to hurt their feelings. Why did Father not say the funeral Mass for my loved one? Why didn't someone from church visit me or one of my sick relatives in the hospital?

People carry a myriad of reasons with them for a lifetime that must eventually be unraveled and worked through before they can reconcile with their Catholic faith. But, a loving and kind invitation is always welcome. These people desperately need kindness, compassion, and empathy — somebody to care for and reach out to them. I don't think they can dig themselves out of the mire they're in by themselves. They need the Good Shepherd to lend a hand to them through us, working on his behalf. We are the hands and feet of Christ! And, although we may not agree with or even understand the reasons for their anger — they truly are needy in spirit. Best to think of them in our Good Shepherd's words: "whatsoever you do for the least of my brethren, that you do unto me" (Matthew 25:40).

## Driven out of the flock

Some feel they've been driven out of the flock. One woman talked about her mother-in-law who stayed away a lifetime, but raised her kids Catholic. She was an orphan. Her mother died when she was very young and she was put in a Catholic orphanage. All she had from her dead mother was her Bible. However, when she was placed in the Catholic orphanage, for some inexplicable reason, the sisters confiscated her mother's Bible and threw it away.

A noted neurosurgeon I met on a plane — when I happened to say I just did a Catholics Returning Home seminar — immediately looked like he was going to cry as he told me he used to be Catholic. He said when he was in medical school and his wife was in nursing school, raising their kids, they wanted to send them to PSR, but in his words, "They didn't have two nickels to rub together." The parish wanted them to pay unaffordable tuition. So, they left and went to a Protestant church where they were warmly received.

Another woman who was away from the Church talked about having a poor childhood and being put in Catholic school. She was left-handed, so the sisters beat her left hand to make her use her right hand. Many people with disabled and/or sick kids talk about the negative experiences they went through when trying to bring their kids to church. Other people were rude to them and told them to leave because their kids were disruptive.

In my own experience, I recall being dirt poor with my abusive alcoholic father and mentally-ill mother, trying to fend for ourselves when I went to Catholic school from fourth to eighth grade. We didn't have anybody feeding or caring for us. One day I picked out an oversized, sleeveless dress to wear to school. The sister made an example of me in front of the class for wearing immoral clothing, because the dress was sleeveless. Then, the kids circled me in the playground, laughing and taunting me and calling me names. I still can hear them laughing at me in the classroom, with sister raising her voice saying I was "disgraceful," and on the playground while they were circling around me.

These are deep hurts and lifelong, crippling, traumatic experiences. In all these cases, we were truly needy at the time of our experiences, and not only did the church people not help us, instead they made our situations worse. But, God the Father has always looked out for the needy and helpless. He sent Jesus, his Son, the Good Shepherd as the role model. In Ezekiel 34, God the Father uses some rather harsh language toward both the shepherds of Israel and the other sheep for mistreating, ignoring, and driving away the weak, wounded, and sick sheep from the rest of the flock.

"Woe to the shepherds of Israel who have been pasturing themselves! Should not shepherds, rather, pasture sheep? ...You did not strengthen the weak nor heal the sick and bind up the injured. You did not bring back the strayed nor seek the lost, but you lorded it over them harshly and brutally. So they were scattered for lack of a shepherd, and became food for all the wild beasts.

"I myself will look after and tend my sheep... The lost I will seek out, the strayed I will bring back, the injured I will bind up, the sick I will heal...

"As for you, my sheep, says the Lord God, I will judge between one sheep and another... Was it not enough for you to graze on the best pasture, that you had to trample the rest of your pastures with your feet? Was it not enough for you to drink the clearest water, that you had to foul the remainder with your feet? Thus my sheep had to graze on what your feet had trampled and drink what your feet had fouled... Now will I judge between the fat and the lean sheep. Because you push with side and shoulder, and butt all the weak sheep with your horns until you have driven them out, I will save my sheep..." (Ezekiel 34:2-4, 11-16, 17-22).

## The Good Shepherd brings back his strays

Many leave the Church simply because they move to a new area and never make the effort to find and join a new parish, or they join a Protestant church where they feel more welcome or at home than they did as a Catholic. Many divorced people are so hurt, ashamed, and embarrassed by their divorce that they don't want to stay at the parish where all their families and friends are. They can't bear to be around everybody who knew them when they were married, because they feel so awkward now that they're divorced and single. So, even though they're not particularly against the Catholic faith and not that committed to a Protestant church, they'll make the move just to make a fresh start.

Some leave the Church when they marry someone from a different religion, a non-believer or someone very anti-Catholic. For many people, it is a very difficult life choice to make, when choosing between a loving companion and their Catholic faith. Yet, the Lord never gives up on them and lovingly follows and calls them, and some eventually come back. I've met quite a few returnees who left the Church and stayed away 30-50 years until their anti-Catholic spouse died. One woman said she was so glad to be back after forty-six years, that she's so sorry for wasting all that time. Now that she's back, she doesn't want to waste one second of her life; she wants to use every moment helping others return. So, she leads a Catholics Returning Home ministry at her winter parish, so she can help as many people as she possibly can during the time she has left.

## Let faith take its course

Many parents are upset when their children no longer attend church and wonder what they can do to bring them back. The answer lies in nonjudgmental acceptance of their children's choices and renewed commitment to their own faith development. We can't make anyone else return to the Church (or do anything else they don't want to do, for that matter)! We can pray for others and lovingly invite them to return, but ultimately the choice is theirs. We can focus on our own walk with the Lord and renew that commitment. If others observe our peace, security, joy, and love of the Lord, they are likely to be drawn to the same source. Faith is caught, not taught, and it can never be forced.

But, we can always invite others and let them know they're welcome to attend or return to the Church. However, the key is to understand the difference of making a nonjudgmental invitation versus becoming a pest, hounding or badgering someone else, especially one's own children. Sometimes it's hard for parents to accept their children as adults who need to stand on their own feet and make their own life choices. Many returnees have said they left the Church precisely because religion was "shoved down their throats" by their parents, and so they rebelled as soon as they left home. If our Father in heaven allows us the freedom to make our own choices in order that we may learn, grow, and develop faith and strength of character in our own timeframe and in our own unique way, then we as earthly parents must strive to do the same. Faith is made stronger when it's allowed the freedom to grow and develop rather than being forced or controlled.

Most people who return to the Church after a long absence are very guilt-ridden, for not having passed on their faith to their children. They agonize over not properly preparing their children for life. In many cases their children are already grown and these parents berate themselves mercilessly for having failed in their parental duties. I tell them that they have an opportunity to make a significant impression on their children, other family members, and acquaintances by the change they make in their own lives. By concentrating on their own faith walk and reveling in their newfound peace, security, and joy in the Lord, others can't help but notice such a change, especially grown children observing their parents.

## Searching for God

Most non-practicing Catholics eventually want to return to the Church due to major life events such as a family crisis, an illness, a marriage, births, deaths, job loss or success, and many other reasons. As people begin to mature and question the paradoxes of life, they begin to search for the stability and peace that only God can provide in the Church community. They say they're missing something in their lives. Saint Augustine said "our hearts are restless until they rest in thee, oh Lord!"

The saying that babies are among the greatest apostles rings true because new parents frequently come back to the Church in order to pass on their faith to their children.

Among the more heartbreaking stories I've heard, from those who have been away from the Church, come from those parents who say they baptized their own children because they didn't think they could return, but they wanted to save their children.

## Some mistakenly think they're excommunicated

A middle-aged dentist called me and asked what he could do to have his new baby and other young children baptized and made part of the Church. He said that he knows he's excommunicated, because he was divorced and remarried, and he didn't get an annulment from his first marriage. He said he doesn't know where to start in coming back to the Church, since he has been away from the Church for over twenty years. He said he prays the Our Father over and over, hoping that God is listening to him. Also, he mentioned that he himself baptized his children, because he's so afraid of approaching the Church, and he didn't want them to be punished because of his failures.

Many non-practicing Catholics would like to return to the Catholic Church; however, they don't know where to start. They are especially concerned about their status in the Church and many mistakenly think they have been excommunicated and are not allowed to come back. They are afraid to approach the Church, for fear of being rejected. It's very difficult for non-practicing Catholics to get their nerve up to make contact with the Church. Thus, for those involved in various points of entry within parish ministries, such as the parish school, PSR, baptismal preparation, and parish registration, it's important to keep in mind what it took for that returning Catholic to show up on their doorstep.

Some will turn to a Protestant church because of the evangelization efforts by many non-Catholic Christian churches, and because most Protestant churches welcome and accept them. In fact, many Protestant churches "target" inactive/non-practicing Catholics in their evangelization efforts. Thus, it is most important to extend a personal invitation from the Catholic Church to welcome non-practicing Catholics back to the Church. They need to feel that the Church wants them back, and will take them back, without putting them through a lot of red tape. "Once a Catholic, always a Catholic — if you want to be" is a saying that I have coined for returning Catholics to assure them they are welcome.

## Accepting adult returnees as they are

Many non-practicing Catholics are unfamiliar with even the most basic beliefs of the Church and are at only a beginning level of understanding of the Catholic faith. Even if they have been educated in the Catholic school system, most of those who have been away from the Church are very confused and mixed-up about Catholic beliefs. Even if they're highly educated and successful in life, many of these non-practicing Catholics are truly children in adult bodies with regard to their understanding of the Catholic faith. It doesn't matter if they are doctors, lawyers, have Ph.D.'s, or are successful millionaires — many returnees are almost childlike when it comes to their concepts and ideas about the Catholic religion.

While presenting a Catholics Returning Home seminar, I had just explained my belief that many returning Catholics are at a grade-school level of understanding of the Catholic faith, and that they even talk about faith and religion in the language of their childhood. A priest raised his hand and said that just the evening before, he had an experience with a returning Catholic that embodied that very reality. The priest said the returning Catholic asked him a question about the Catholic faith that was so naïve that he was amazed an educated adult would even consider such a question. So, to make a point, the priest asked the man if he, as a forty-five-year-old, still believed and followed what his mother told him about sex when he was in grade school. His mother's teachings about sex in grade school was appropriate at the time, but certainly not for use as a mature adult. The priest told the man that it's the same with the teachings about the Catholic faith. The Catholic faith needs to be viewed through the lens of adulthood, rather than understood at the grade-school level.

## Getting up the nerve to come

Many people who have attended Catholics Returning Home sessions have said they attempted to come to an earlier series, but were afraid to get out of the car. Instead, they sat in the parking lot. Others say they got lost on the church grounds, trying to find the room where the meetings were being held. It's important to have signs up and team members directing people to where the meetings are going to be held. Some say they've watched the signs for CRH for several years before calling, because they were afraid. Many who call for information about Catholics Returning Home are very hesitant and fearful, and some will say they're calling on behalf of someone else. Some attendees have said they're attending the sessions on behalf of someone else. It's important to accept everyone at face value and allow them their "cover," if that's what they need to feel comfortable in the group.

One man who attended a six-week series said he was attending on behalf of his wife who had scheduling conflicts. He would preface every single comment with, "My wife would say this..." or "My wife feels this way..." or "My wife left because of...." It soon became apparent that he was the real author of those comments. Even though he attended every one of the six sessions, he never changed his stance. He continued to be resolute that he was attending on behalf of his wife.

## Miraculous transformations

But all of this awkwardness, hesitancy, and fear displayed by returning Catholics is normal. It's all part of the process. The first step is often the most difficult for these people to make, which is to get up the nerve to call or come to the sessions. But, once they start attending the series and get more comfortable with the team and learn more about the Church, their fears and defenses dissipate. It's amazing how they change over the six weeks from scared rabbits to relaxed, calm, comfortable people among friends, all through the grace of the Lord working in their hearts! He alone is the inspiration, peace, and stability that they are desperately seeking to heal their longing souls. And, the team members are truly the instruments of grace for this marvelous transformation to take place.

## Chapter 2

# Overview and Key Elements of the Catholics Returning Home Program

## The Prodigal Son

Jesus said to them:

"A man had two sons. The younger of them said to his father, 'Father, give me the share of the estate that is coming to me.' So the father divided up the property. Some days later this younger son collected all his belongings and went off to a distant land, where he squandered his money on dissolute living. After he had spent everything, a great famine broke out in that country and he was in dire need. So he attached himself to one of the propertied class of the place, who sent him to his farm to take care of the pigs. He longed to fill his belly with the husks that were fodder for the pigs, but no one made a move to give him anything. Coming to his senses at last, he said: 'How many hired hands at my father's place have more than enough to eat, while here I am starving! I will break away and return to my father, and say to him, "Father, I have sinned against God and against you; I no longer deserve to be called your son. Treat me like one of your hired hands."' With that he set off for his father's house. While he was still a long way off, his father caught sight of him and was deeply moved. He ran out to meet him, threw his arms around his neck, and kissed him. The son said to him, 'Father, I have sinned against God and against you; I no longer deserve to be called your son.' The father said to his servants: 'Quick! Bring out the finest robe and put it on him; put a ring on his finger and shoes on his feet. Take the fatted calf and kill it. Let us eat and celebrate because this son of mine was dead and has come back to life. He was lost and is found.' Then the celebration began" (Luke 15:11-24).

## Origins

My program draws on the late Fr. William McKee's and Msgr. Thomas Cahalane's programs for reaching out to inactive Catholics, and the twelve-step programs I've attended: Adult Children of Alcoholics (ACoA) and Al-Anon for families and friends of alcoholics. But, mostly, I've relied on my own first-hand experience of being an angry, alienated Catholic and have developed a very simple, practical, parish-based program that is time tested and proven.

## Twelve-step roots

Adult Children of Alcoholics (ACoA) and Al-Anon group meetings are for families of alcoholics or drug addicts. These meetings are support groups for these families in order to help them deal with the aftermath of living around people who abuse alcohol and/or drugs. The meetings are very supportive and affirming. They follow a twelve-step program, where the first step is to acknowledge there's a higher power (God) and turn your life over to him. I observed that most people who have lived through the dysfunction and trauma of alcoholism within the family abandoned the practice of their religion. Families of alcoholics and/or drug addicts typically become so traumatized and dysfunctional that their lives become chaotic and disordered to the point that certain normal activities, such as attending church, are discarded. It is fitting, therefore, that the first step in the path toward recovery in twelve-step programs is to re-establish contact with one's higher power or God and eventually to some type of organized religion.

During my struggle to reconcile with my higher power or God, I found it to be very difficult to relate to much of the religious symbolism concerning images of God and family. If your natural father is abusive, violent, and cruel, it's very difficult to imagine a loving, caring, and kind God who is "father." Much of the religious imagery associated with the Church talks of a loving, forgiving family life — which is the exact opposite of the dynamic of an alcoholic family. If your mother, father, sisters, and brothers are angry, hostile, spiteful, and vindictive amongst themselves and to others, it's almost impossible to imagine a God or faith community that is loving and forgiving. If you're brought up to be shamed, chastised, and constantly told that you're worthless from early on in life, it's almost impossible to change your self-concept to one of self-love and acceptance. If your family of origin has been chaotic and abusive, it's difficult to develop trust in a church family.

## Spiritual desolation is poorest of the poor

Thus, a person who grew up in a dysfunctional family is at a severe disadvantage in learning to trust and belong in a faith community. As part of the twelve-step process, one is encouraged to rely on the group itself as their faith community, because most twelve-steppers are totally adrift and removed from any sort of organized religion or personal faith. Most of these folks are truly destitute, spiritually needy, and barely hanging on to any sort of spiritual beliefs. They are truly the poorest of the poor in their faith life and in their ties to organized religion. The abuse of alcohol or drugs has wreaked havoc and ravaged their family life and plunged most of these people into despair.

Dysfunctional families are very common. There are no perfect families. So many people have been affected by alcoholism, drugs, and other stressful issues, such as mental and/or physical illness in their families. I'm always amazed at how many people tell me that they come from dysfunctional families. It is important to remember, when conducting the Catholics Returning Home program, that many people returning to the Church have some type of dysfunction in their family which they are attempting to deal with in their adult lives.

What I really like about the entire twelve-step process is that it's geared to accept people where they're at, no matter how destitute or hopeless they may be. There is hope for everyone no matter how bad the situation, because people can always seek and gain the grace of God as they strive to change and improve. In the Gospels, Jesus accepted people wherever they were spiritually or psychologically, but he always called them to more. He purposefully sought out the outcasts, sinners, and rejects from the organized religion of his day. He was criticized and ridiculed for spending his time with such people. He offered them forgiveness and hope, no matter what they had done. Thus, Catholics Returning Home is modeled after Jesus' invitation to and acceptance of all, no matter what they've done or not done — because no one is beyond the mercy of God. Jesus walked amongst known sinners and welcomed them back — we as his disciples can do no less.

## Cheap, easy, and effective

I developed and refined the Catholics Returning Home program by trial and error over time. It includes what is absolutely the bare minimum requirements so as to accomplish the objective of reaching out to people who are away from their Catholic faith and helping them return and reconcile with the Church, while providing them with a working knowledge of Catholicism and a safe place to vent their frustrations in a healing, affirming manner with the least cost and effort. In other words, "cheap, easy, and effective," with the content being plain, vanilla Catholic, so that the basics are covered in a simple, practical, understandable manner for adult beginners. Every step and component part that I have kept in the program meets those requirements.

When followed as designed, Catholics Returning Home miraculously draws in people who are a long way off, some like scared rabbits initially, and in the period of six weeks, they're transformed into relaxed, calm, laid back disciples, eager and hungry for more faith formation and development, and ready to seek out other faith sharing opportunities in the parish. It works like a charm and is awesome to behold!

## The name of "Catholics Returning Home"

The name "Catholics Returning Home" is anointed. It perfectly describes the ministry. Somehow with the Lord's grace, it captures and touches the hearts of people who are completely estranged, alienated, and a long way off. It lovingly calls them to return to their Catholic faith. It's miraculous!

Over and over I've heard people tell similar stories about how they decided to attend the Catholics Returning Home ministry after seeing the signs out and about. They say they knew immediately what it was and that it was for them. Some say they watched the signs for years before acting. Others say they started out by making the Sign of the Cross when going by, and then gradually got their nerve up to call.

Every word in the name is meaningful. The first word being "Catholics," to grab all Catholics attention. The second word "Returning" puts the onus on the Catholic who is away, that they have to take action and make the effort. We're putting out the signs and publicity, but it's on the returnees' plate to do something about it and make the choice to act. And, the final word "Home" says it all. It means coming back where they belong, where they started out, where they're always welcome, where they're among family who love them and where they're accepted warts and all. For marketing purposes, it's a perfect fit because it describes what the ministry is and it captures the attention of the target market. Thus, the name "Catholics Returning Home" is a critical element of the ministry. Truly, it is the Lord who works miracles in those three words because Jesus said, "No one can come to me unless the Father who sent me draws him" (John 6:44).

## The timing of the series is critical

Catholics Returning Home is designed to have three major outreaches per year, when we have the greatest chance of attracting the attention of people who are returning to the Church for Christmas, Easter, and in the fall. For most parishes, these are the times of the year when it seems that returning Catholics are most open to an invitation to return. Thus, the advertising publicity is put out before Christmas and Easter and in August, and the actual six-week series starts after Christmas and Easter and in mid-September. However, for some parishes where people come for the winter or summer, it makes sense to offer Catholics Returning Home when the returnees are there and seeking.

Since the objective is to reach out and attract the attention of those returning Catholics interested in coming back, it makes sense to offer the series on their timeframe, when they're interested. Otherwise, you will put in a lot of work and end up with few or no attendees. Some parishes offer Catholics Returning Home once or twice a year, rather than three times, based on the time of year they're most successful at attracting returning Catholics.

## A special needs healing ministry

The six-week series is constructed to be welcoming, healing, and compassionate with a focus on basic-level updates of the essentials of the Catholic faith. Thus, the content and order of the six-weeks are important. The first two weeks are designed to be a managed support group, where there are clear boundaries to create a safe, healing environment where people can share their stories and vent in a format that is not combative and antagonistic.

It's important in this type of gathering with potentially angry, alienated people, that we adhere to firm, clear boundaries and objectives, to maintain an orderly and safe environment. Thus, the first two weeks have an agenda that is to be closely followed to accomplish our objective, to help people share and vent, without having a complete grudge fest of displaced rage and hostility that nobody would want to attend. By sticking to the agenda in a seamless manner without looking contrived, the attendees relax, open up, and share more. Thus, your team can avert arguments or getting into heated, unanswerable, and controversial topics that nobody can win.

## The group is positive, healing, and uplifting

The design of Catholics Returning Home includes the principles of "tough love" from the support group programs I've attended. This means that we welcome returnees and accept them with compassion, kindness, and love. However, we will maintain sufficient structure and boundaries within the group through the use of an agenda or syllabus, so that everyone is treated with dignity and respect, especially members of the team, priests, deacons, and lay presenters. By utilizing the anonymous questionnaires, returnees can vent on paper instead of unloading on others. Venting and sharing is managed by following the agenda so that the group doesn't end up in a bare-fisted brawl. Managing the group in an effort to keep the mood positive is healing and uplifting for all concerned, because if the group ends up being a total complaint session, nobody will want to come back — including the team members.

During the first two weeks, the team is helping these returnees work through their hurts and disappointments with the Church. It truly is the work of Jesus by being present for them. Most have a "church story" and underneath a big bundle of hurts. They come as they are, many with burdens, wounds and disappointments, and of course the "church story" is mixed in with the rest of their lives. The team's role is to listen with kindness and compassion. Of course, many times the stories seem to be jumbled up and almost nonsensical how they could end up blaming the Church for this or that, but it doesn't matter because it's their reality. By being present and accepting to them, we're in the footsteps of Jesus, the great healer, and he is able to lift their burdens and set them free! What a privilege and joy it is to see this miracle happen. Truly, Catholics Returning Home is a special needs, healing ministry in action!

## Topical updates of the Catholic faith

The last four weeks of the series are topical basics of Catholicism:

Week 3: The Church Today Since Vatican II — What's going on and where do you fit in?

Week 4: Explanation of the Mass

Week 5: Tips on Sinning: Explanation of the Sacrament of Reconciliation

Week 6: Explanation/Sharing of the Creed

These four topics should be presented in a simple manner to update the returnees and help them achieve a working knowledge of the Catholic faith. The entire six-week process is designed to allow returnees to share and be listened to and accepted, and then to be open to more faith formation and development.

The sessions are designed to last for an hour and a half. The actual time depends on the customs and schedules of your locality. Some have it 6:30 to 8:00 p.m. and others have it 7:30 to 9:00 p.m. Whatever works in the locality. Most places have the sessions during the evenings from Sunday to Thursday. Weekends usually don't work. However, a few places have had the sessions on Sunday afternoon or evenings.

## The team members

You will need two to five team members. The most important characteristic is to be compassionate and non-judgmental. They don't have to be mini-theologians but they do need to be comfortable and grounded in their faith. It's good to have some people on the team who have been away, but don't worry if you don't have them right away because over time you'll attract them from the actual returning Catholics who decide to help with the ministry after they've went through the series.

Most other ministries in the Church are run by the same small group of "worn-out" people in a particular parish. However, Catholics Returning Home brings people back who have been totally separated, and then allows them to become team leaders and use their experience of being away to help themselves and others return to active membership. Catholics Returning Home is one of those rare efforts within the Church that continually attracts new team members and regenerates its ministerial team. Frequently, those who do return to the Church by way of this program get very involved in activities within the parish. There are some who returned through Catholics Returning Home who became priests or deacons.

## Meeting location

You'll need a comfortable, easy to find room to have the sessions, with access to a DVD player to show the videos during the sessions. The room should have privacy, so that people can feel comfortable to share. A noisy, open gym isn't conducive to the ministry, especially if there are sports or crowds nearby in the same big room.

Some parishes have tried holding the sessions in people's homes to make the returnees feel more comfortable. My feeling is that it's best to have the series at a parish, so the returnees get used to coming back to a church and so they feel that it's the "church" that wants them back. By having it in people's homes, some feel they're being slighted and brought in through the back door.

## A healing journey of faith

Some folks ask, What is the "success rate" of Catholics Returning Home? I would counter by saying, What is the value of one person coming back to the Church? How can we measure the change in that person's life or the contribution that one person makes by being an active member of the community?

We've had a very low drop-out rate in the actual sessions because we made a point of getting to know the returnees individually, talking with them after the sessions, calling them, and trying to make them feel comfortable about joining our group and our parish community. Usually, those who dropped out of the sessions had some scheduling conflicts that interfered with their attending the complete series. However, many would return to a later series. Some would attend off and on for years, because they felt comfortable and at home with the group. It's best to let returnees proceed in their own timeframe without undue pressure. Some return right away and others take years to decide. Ultimately, it is their choice if and when they're going to re-join the church.

If a particular Catholics Returning Home group is experiencing a high drop-out rate, or if the returnees aren't staying and joining the Church, it's important to evaluate how welcoming and accepting your team is. Take a good look at how the returnees are being treated. Ask yourself if you would want to join this particular group or parish community.

## Getting the word out

Publicity is key for this ministry. Because most parishes operate on a tight budget, I've designed Catholics

Returning Home to use as much inexpensive publicity as possible. I've written up all the publicity needed, so all you have to do is insert your parish information and dates. (See the chapter on publicity for details.)

Publicity includes: bulletin articles and inserts, flyers, brochures, Prayers of the Faithful, announcements, outside signs and banners, and if your budget permits, paid ads. The purpose of the parish publicity is to encourage parishioners to give the information to their non-practicing family and friends and bring them to the sessions. The more publicity the better. In spreading the word, no publicity is wasted. Just by seeing the advertising publicity, some will just start attending Mass again and others will bring their children to be baptized or register them to attend PSR or the school proper.

The number of attendees depends on how many Catholics are in the area, how much publicity is gotten out, and if the timing of the series is done when the returning Catholics are open to an invitation and seeking. That is for most parishes after Christmas, Easter, and in the fall, and for vacation spots it's during the winter or summer when the visitors are there with time on their hands. Some parishes get as high as thirty people at a series. Others get 10-15 per series, depending on how they get the publicity out. Smaller areas get less than five attendees per series.

## Our treasure follows our hearts

Most inactive Catholics are open to an invitation to return to the Church if it's done in a kind, compassionate, nonjudgmental manner. Nagging, chasing, and hounding an inactive Catholic will not work to bring someone back. In fact, it will drive them away all the more. Accusing someone of abandoning the Faith or of being immoral or evil will never work. Chastising someone for not contributing to the Church will not work. Our treasure frequently follows our hearts. Thus, if someone isn't paying money to the Church, it's because their heart isn't with the Church. If their hearts are touched by the Lord, their minds, bodies, souls, and even pocketbooks will follow. Catholics Returning Home must never be built on asking the returnees back for their contributions. However, if they are welcomed back and treated compassionately and kindly, many are so touched that they generously give of themselves including their time, treasure, and talent.

## A ministry of compassion rather than law

Catholics Returning Home ministry is one of compassion rather than law. Jesus was a tremendously compassionate person. He refused mercy to no one. He put people first over law. When deciding whether to heal someone on the Sabbath or to be concerned about following the law, he chose to put people first by healing the person in need. He remained on the side of compassion. How do we apply Jesus' teaching to our modern day

Catholic Church and specifically to Catholics who are in the process of returning? Can we invite people back to the Church if they're living in situations that are at odds with Church law? It's one thing to talk about Jesus and quote Scripture and quite another to deal with the realities of Church law.

The answer is always compassion first. All of us are sinners and have fallen short of perfection. The Church is filled with sinners, so we always have room for one more! Only God can judge us and read our hearts and souls. We are called to commit others to the mercy of God who alone knows them and loves them with a father's love. If Jesus the Good Shepherd leaves the ninety-nine and searches out and seeks the one who has strayed and brings that one back to the flock, how can we turn that person away? If the very angels in heaven are rejoicing over the return of that one, shouldn't we be doing the same?

Frequently, team members are concerned about the status of the divorced who have remarried, and they wonder how can we invite them back to the Catholic Church? Very simple, everyone is welcome to return and attend Mass and prayer services. People living in second marriages should be referred to the annulment/divorce ministry within the parish to work through their particular circumstances. In the meantime, however, they're welcome to attend the Catholics Returning Home program and other ministries within the parish.

In speaking with returnees who have been divorced and remarried, one must be gentle and sensitive when discussing their status with them. I tell them that all the

Church laws and rules are still in place, but there is nothing they can't work through with the help of the Lord.

## A hospital emergency room for returning Catholics

Catholics Returning Home sessions can be likened to the emergency room of a hospital in that content should be kept at a more general level to meet the needs of the entire group. For specific needs such as individual help with annulments, bereavement, or other issues, those folks should be routed to the various specialized ministries within the parish. In conducting a Catholics Returning Home program, you will need to know the channels — offices, names, phone numbers, addresses — in order to route people who need to discuss the specific circumstances of divorce/remarriage/annulment, bereavement, and other needs, with a knowledgeable and caring representative of the Church. Based on my experience, there are some identifiable subgroups of returnees: about a third of the returnees are concerned with divorce/remarriage; about a third are grieving because of the death, illness, or disability of loved ones; and while most returnees are disillusioned or somewhat disenchanted with the Church, only a small number are really intensely angry or hostile.

Another subgroup of returnees is former religious which includes former seminarians, sisters, brothers, and resigned priests. While the majority of former religious are able to successfully move back into secular life and maintain a good relationship with the Church, some are not. Many of the former religious I've encountered in Catholics Returning Home were troubled, abandoned, and alienated. For some reason, these folks fell through the cracks and became isolated and adrift from the Church. Most of them wouldn't identify themselves as former religious in the group. They would only identify themselves as such in private, one-on-one meetings or telephone conversations. Many had a lot of guilt and wondered if there was a place for them in the Church. All you can do is assure them they're welcome and they can fit it.

## Building bridges of faith

In racially and/or culturally diverse parishes, it's best to have team members from the various groups. Having separate programs for each group seems to be a waste of resources and is more divisive than unifying. There are many types of exclusivity within our faith communities that must be addressed and rectified. All methods of screening out and marginalizing must be confronted and eliminated, if we are to truly follow Jesus' example of welcoming all. Each parish has its own unique challenges. Whether it concerns social class, income, race, sexual orientation, religion, or the lack of religion, all types of exclusivity must be challenged and replaced with welcoming outreach. Keep in mind that if your parish extends an invitation to all, you must be ready and willing for "all" to accept that invitation.

Those who return are of all ages and come from very different backgrounds. Like the emergency room of a hospital, anyone can walk in the door. Catholics Returning Home's philosophy is to welcome everybody, no matter what level they are at, and make sure that activities and content are geared toward those who are the most needy. The content and structure are designed to welcome back the most fragile and skeptical, because the others who are more confident or assured will also be comfortable if the most needy are cared for.

As noted earlier, most of the returnees are at a grade-school level in their understanding of Catholicism. They may be highly educated and successful in their lives and careers, but they are usually at stage one concerning Catholicism. This is not to say they don't have faith or belief in God. Many are prayerful and have a very strong and positive faith life. Most have a good relationship with God, but may have a negative opinion of the Church.

Some have tried other religions, especially Protestant Christian churches. In fact, some return because they become offended when representatives of the Protestant church they are attending starts criticizing the Catholic Church. For many of these returning Catholics, those criticisms by the Protestant church toward Catholicism awaken their faith in and love for the Catholic Church. When some people start attending Protestant churches, that may be the quickest way to reawaken their faith and love for the Catholic Church. When the Protestant church starts to go against the grain of a Catholicism so deeply rooted, many ricochet back to the Faith.

## Continued faith development

It's important to have ongoing adult education and small-group faith-sharing ministries within a parish in order to route returnees in their continued faith development. Many returnees want to continue the series beyond the six weeks. This is a wonderful affirmation of just how well a Catholics Returning Home Program can "work" — to bring someone back into the fold who felt totally separated from the Church, and in the space of six weeks to have that person experience such a transformation that they want to continue their development within the Church — this is truly the work of the Spirit. You will need to help the returnees navigate other opportunities for faith development within your parish or area, so they can continue their lifelong faith journey. They've only just begun!

## Chapter 3

# Basic Program Requirements for Starting Catholics Returning Home

## A welcoming place is necessary

If we look to the Parable of the Prodigal Son (Luke 15:11-32), the returning son was welcomed, fully restored to his position as son, and his family threw a party for him and had a huge celebration. And, in the Parable of the Lost Sheep (Luke 15:4-7), Jesus the Good Shepherd speaks of leaving the ninety-nine and searching out the one who strayed, and bringing it back to the fold. The angels of heaven rejoiced over the return of the one who had strayed. As disciples, we need to model these parables when we're helping Catholics return. Returning Catholics need to feel welcomed, missed, and that they belong. They need to know they have a "place" in the Church. They need to be listened to, without being judged as being unforgivable sinners. With Catholics Returning Home, they have their own group where they can safely vent and share their stories without being ignored or dismissed.

Catholics Returning Home needs to be held in a welcoming, hospitable parish in order to work as designed. Both the pastor and the faith community need to be open and supportive to having returning Catholics come back into their midst. I've been at parishes where either the pastoral staff or the community complained about having all the returnees clogging up the parking lots, and in the church taking their favorite spots. Or, that it was too much work catching up the returnees' kids on sacramental preparation and/or the parents on adult faith and annulments.

One upscale parish where I started Catholics Returning Home complained about the outside signs and bulletin articles, because they couldn't understand why we should put so much effort into these lowlife deadbeats rather than taking care of the needs of the regular paying members. Some people have told me that when they tried to get Catholics Returning Home started at their parishes, they were told by the pastoral staff that they couldn't put up signs and disrupt the other activities in the parish. So, I advised them to look to Jesus the Good Shepherd as our model in Matthew 10:14, "If anyone does not receive you or listen to what you have to say, leave that house or town, and once outside it shake its dust from your feet." And then, go find another parish that is open and welcoming to returning Catholics, because obviously the ministry isn't going to work if the parish and pastoral staff aren't supportive. In particular because returnees are so sensitive to slight, they'll pick up those vibes immediately and leave. But don't worry, the Lord prepares the way for his work to be done. When he closes a door, he often opens a window for his wonderful grace, mercy, and love to flow!

## Pastor and parish support of ministry

In order to start Catholics Returning Home ministry in a parish, you'll have to have permission from the pastor and/or parish council and related committee that is responsible for adult faith. Make sure the pastor and parish administrative structure have approved of and fully support the Catholics Returning Home program.

In many parishes, you will need to meet with the respective committee and even the parish council to explain what the program entails, why it is needed, and how it relates to the parish's overall goals and objectives. You will also need to provide an estimate of the cost of implementing and running the program. The cost is minimal and primarily depends on the decision to invest in books, videos, outdoor signs and banners, flyers, brochures, and ads. They need to commit to providing the necessary budget and support for the program. They also need to "buy into" helping spread the word for outreach, welcoming them, and being prepared to accept them back into the parish. The returnees will bring back their entire families, which means catching up for the spouse and kids, and there may be annulment issues to work through. The pastor and the administrative structure can work wonders in gaining support from the rest of the parish by setting the proper welcoming environment. The pastor doesn't have to have much "hands-on" day to day involvement for the program to succeed, but if he is vocal in his support of the program and the people who serve it, Catholics Returning Home can flourish in that parish.

## Two to five people on the team

The team should have two to five members and one person should be in charge to keep the group focused and on track. If the community is racially or culturally diverse, the team should have representatives from the different groups. Avoid selecting those who are overcommitted and on every church committee. Catholics Returning Home needs team members who have a calling specific to this ministry and the time and commitment to devote to it. This program is an "up-close and personal" ministry. Frequently, team members form lifelong bonds and friendships with returnees, so they should be willing to have that kind of closeness or intimacy with them.

It's not necessary that team members have "heavy duty" theological backgrounds. However, they should be comfortable with their own faith. The most important trait of team members is the ability to accept returnees where they're at, without judging them or wanting to fix them or remake them into their own image. This usually takes someone who is relatively comfortable with themselves and their own faith journey. Personality types to avoid are those who are rigid, black and white legalistic types, who want to "save those big sinners." Best to avoid people who have an agenda to promote some other ministry over everything else. For example, if they have a specific cause or apostolate and they want to get in front of any church group they can to convince them to join whatever they're promoting. Returning Catholics don't need to be further confused by the inner competing groups within the church. It's great to have a mixture of returnees as well as those who have never left.

Don't worry if you don't have returnees on the team initially, because you will get them as Catholics Returning Home is held. Although it may seem to border on the ridiculous to ask someone to help with the next outreach when they themselves have recently returned, it's actually very beneficial to all concerned. Helping others return to the Church is very healing for those recently returned. It is also very inspirational for newcomers to see others who have been back only a short time, already bursting with enthusiasm and zeal to share the good news. Returnees find it very affirming to be trusted enough to be on the team, and they are frequently the most dynamic and enthusiastic members. Of course they shouldn't be given team responsibilities that are beyond their abilities, but at a minimum they could share their stories and help with some of the footwork.

Sometimes people are concerned, after a few years of having Catholics Returning Home, that they're getting too many team members. One option is to divide the team up into smaller parts so that each group works on one six-week series per year, so your teams are alternated and have a break. Everybody can still help with the publicity outreach work.

The team should work on developing their listening skills. Listening means being present, paying attention to and accepting someone else's comments. Returning Catholics are very confused and have minimal understanding of the Catholic faith. Thus, sometimes, they voice some rather strange, uninformed thoughts and opinions about Catholicism. Don't argue with them at this point; just allow them to say what they feel. Even if you were to win such an argument, you would risk losing any number of returnees and turning them off to the Church. Sometimes, they may purposely say ridiculous and controversial things just to mask their insecurity or lack of knowledge of the Catholic faith. Try to find something to agree with in whatever they say, or tell them that's interesting or that it's another point of view. Usually if you accept them and agree with them — at least on some point of common ground — they're satisfied. During the sessions, stick to the agenda items and try not to bring in any other topics or issues so as to avoid "opening up a can of worms." Team members can talk with the returnees individually after the sessions or in a phone conversation to discuss their personal situations and answer open-ended questions one-on-one.

Team members need to realize that they're not supposed to chase down and "fix" returnees, or that they have to know everything and have answers to every question or detail that comes up, especially within the actual sessions. During the first two sessions, the team needs to understand their role in keeping the group on track and not going off onto tangents and opening up controversial issues. It's important for the team members to be willing to open up and share some of their own personal stories, without monopolizing with their personal details. They need to be able to do this naturally, without making it look forced or contrived — this helps returnees feel more comfortable. They need to keep the focus on helping the returnees.

During the group process and sharing of the first two weeks of the series, the returnees and the team bond to form a small, close-knit faith community anchored by trust. For returning Catholics, the team is their link or tie with the Church. The small-group faith community is "church" to the returning Catholics. It is the place where they are accepted, welcomed, listened to without being judged. The same team members need to commit for the six-week series for continuity and stability. In cases where several parishes join together to do Catholics Returning Home, you should have one parish take responsibility for continuity with the same team for the six-week series. Otherwise, you'll have a high dropout rate. All the team members should read and study this "how-to" book so everybody is clear on the objective and their specific roles.

## Team members as sheepdogs

A good example to think about as to how the team should handle returning Catholics is like "sheepdogs." I happened to see "sheepdog trials" on TV and I was fascinated by their dedication and precision in herding sheep from one place to another. The Gospel images of Jesus the Good Shepherd are so powerful and meaningful, especially if you look closer at shepherds, sheep, and sheepdogs. Sheep are harmless, gentle, helpless, tame little animals that even vocalize in such plaintive, heart-rending bleats. They sound like they need help! Shepherds carefully pasture and care for these helpless little animals because they can't take care of themselves. And, then there are these adorable, gentle, cute, single-minded sheepdogs who do the shepherd's bidding to guard and herd the sheep to safety.

In watching the sheepdog trials, I was struck how on the shepherd's signal, a low whistle, soft command or gesture, these adorable little sheepdogs will quickly run to surround the sheep and gently but firmly nudge the sheep to go in a specific direction. If the sheep are going the right direction, the sheepdogs will quietly lie down and watch them intently. However, as soon as the sheep veer off course, the sheepdogs quickly spring up and surround them to put them right back on course. The sheepdogs work together seamlessly as a team and they all know their jobs. And, above all, the sheepdogs don't harm or scatter the sheep. Instead, they work in perfect unison to move the sheep to the gate and safety.

Thus, Sheepdogs, you all know your objective in bringing back our lost sheep! As a team, you need to study how this ministry works, figure out who does what to get the work done, and then during the series, everybody does their jobs as seamlessly as possible without sounding contrived or rehearsed, and it works like a charm! The objective is to gather in the sheep without scattering or running them off!

## Catholics Returning Home and the RCIA

We worked in the RCIA ministry for many years before starting Catholics Returning Home. RCIA is for people who haven't had the sacraments of initiation: Baptism, Holy Eucharist, and Confirmation including non-Catholic Christians. Some parishes put returning Catholics into the RCIA group without having a separate program for returning Catholics. Most parishes don't allow returning Catholics in the RCIA because they've already had their sacraments of initiation.

Many returning Catholics have some degree of anger and hostility toward the Church; whereas, the people becoming Catholic are coming in with minimal prior experience of the Catholic Church. Returning Catholics in an RCIA group tend to feel out of place, because they're not included in any of the RCIA ceremonies and rituals. Many say they feel almost jealous that newcomers are given all this attention and special treatment, while they are excluded and can only observe as onlookers. They say they feel like second-class citizens or displaced foster children who are brought in through the back door. Most returning Catholics prefer to remain private, so they can proceed at their own pace, in their own way. Plus, people becoming Catholic in the RCIA tend to get impatient and frustrated with some of the returning Catholics' negative emotions.

The Catholics Returning Home ministry, through the Lord's grace, excels at casting the nets in the deep waters and bringing back an assorted catch, many who are still a long way off. Thus, sometimes, the people responding to the outreach publicity haven't had all their sacraments of initiation and they do fit into the RCIA. However, it's best to let them attend and proceed through the Catholics Returning Home series without moving them around elsewhere, until they get comfortable and settled back in Church. Many returnees are skittish and uncertain about their status in the Church and they are particularly sensitive to being shuffled around and mixed in with another group of strangers. Therefore, it's best to let RCIA candidates attend the six-week series and then route them to the RCIA as the next step in their conversion journey, on their timeframe when they're ready.

Sometimes RCIA teams can get a little persnickety about the Catholics Returning Home ministry stealing their sheep. However, keep in mind that these returnees were lost sheep scattered far and wide, and if it hadn't been for the Lord's grace working through the Catholics Returning Home ministry, they would still be scattered in the brambles and wasteland. Thus, patience is the watchword in this instance, and in due time, these lost sheep will be routed back to the fold through the RCIA as the next step in their faith journey when they are ready.

## Meeting times and room location

The sessions should be an hour and a half, usually during the evenings of Sunday to Thursday. In most parishes, meeting space is at a premium. You have to work with the resources and facilities available in a particular parish. That said, you should try to have the meetings at a comfortable, easy to find room. And, it's great if possible to have the meetings in or near the church so that you can close each session saying the Our Father around the altar. Since the sessions are rather intense and emotional, you need to have some privacy. Avoid having the sessions in a large open gym with sporting events going on in the same area.

One parish in a Chicago suburb asked me to visit their sessions to determine why they had such a high dropout rate. Would you want to attend a Catholics Returning Home session with a screaming, noisy sports crowd on the other end of the gym? In addition, at this parish, they had some people that were "observers" who were not part of the group, but they just wanted to watch and observe what the returnees were like and what they were talking about. Sort of like observing insects under a microscope or lab rats in a cage? Is it any wonder that this Catholics Returning Home group ran amok and didn't last for long?

At another Chicago suburb parish where I helped them get started, I arrived when it was already dark. The parish looked really dark with lots of buildings, so I drove around a couple times looking for the meeting location. Finally, just by chance, I saw a light shining through an open door, and looking closer, I saw a small piece of paper hung on the outside. So, I got out of my car, walked up to the door and sure enough, the door was wedged open and there was a small half sheet of paper advertising Catholics Returning Home. So, I carefully let myself in making sure to keep the door wedged open, so it wouldn't lock behind me. Then I walked and walked through corridors with small pieces of paper placed here and there until finally I arrived in a small "adult faith" library. And there were all the Catholics Returning Home team members sitting at the table, patiently waiting for the returnees to arrive. I asked them if anyone was outside patrolling the parking lot — and of course no one was. So, I told them I'm going back outside to look for returnees. My husband usually does this job when we're running our sessions. So, three times I brought people back to the library until I couldn't find any more outside. Who knows how many we missed because they got lost and gave up and left! Moral of the story: Sheepdogs have to help the lost sheep find their way!

## Timing of the six-week series

"He said to Simon, 'Put out into deep water and lower your nets for a catch.' Simon answered, 'Master, we have been hard at it all night long and have caught nothing; but if you say so, I will lower the nets.' Upon doing this they caught such a great number of fish that their nets were at the breaking point. They signaled to their mates in the other boat to come and help them. These came, and together they filled the two boats until they nearly sank…Jesus said to Simon, 'Do not be afraid. From now on you will be catching men'" (Luke 5:4-10).

Saint Peter started out as a fisherman, who became a great apostle and fisher of men after answering the Lord's call. He knew the toils and trials of trying to catch fish. Even when toiling all night long in deep water with nets, they still got skunked and came up short. But, when Jesus told them to put down the nets, they filled their nets so full that they almost sank their boats. That's a fisherman's dream. But, the key was Saint Peter faithfully doing what Jesus told him to do.

## We're fishing to catch fish

We too are fishers of men and women. That's what Catholics Returning Home ministry is all about, fishing for those who are adrift and lost at sea. But, we're fishing to catch fish. We want to bring them in. We're fishing for those who are open to and responding to the Lord's call. It's the Lord who has worked in their hearts and spirits to tenderly and lovingly beckon them to return to him. We are the instruments through which the Lord works. Saint Mother Teresa said she was the pencil in the Lord's hands, as we are.

For most parishes, at Christmas and Easter, we experience a huge influx of people who have been away. We call them Chreesters because we see them only a couple times per year. We see some of them at weddings, funerals, registering their kids at PSR, Catholic school, or Baptism preparation. We see some returning in the fall when PSR and school starts and for RCIA inquiry outreach. In these instances, it is the Lord touching their hearts and drawing them in. It is on their timeframe, not ours. Therefore, since the Master called them and they responded, we as good fishers of people need to put out our nets when they're back in church seeking. We need to be kind to them when they're here and invite them to more. That's what Catholics Returning Home is all about. Thus, the timing of having the Catholics Returning Home outreach publicity and the actual six-week series is tailored to meet the needs of those we're serving, those who are away and may be open to returning.

The publicity and outreach are designed to occur during Lent up until Easter, when they're in our churches where we invite them to join us for the six-week series starting after Easter. It's the same with Advent and Christmas. The publicity outreach goes out during Advent up until Christmas, when the church is full and we invite them to join us for the six-week series beginning in January. And, for the fall, the publicity outreach is done during August and September, with the six-week series starting in mid-September. This design works the best to put the nets out when the fish are there and biting, because we're fishing to catch fish. If you don't adhere to this timing, you're probably going to end up just fishing without catching any fish. Like Saint Peter before Jesus' intervention, you could be "hard at it all night long and catch nothing" (Luke 5:5).

For parishes located where people migrate to spend the winter or summer months, you have an opportunity to catch the fish when they're there and biting. Many of them have time on their hands and they actually feel more comfortable returning to the church away from their permanent home where they have more privacy and anonymity. Some parishes in these areas offer continuous back to back six-week series when the visitors are there. They keep their publicity and advertising out for six months during the visitor/vacation season. Some summer vacation spots offer the six sessions twice a week for three weeks to get them when they're there. For parishes located in northern climates, many don't do Catholics Returning Home in the winter months. For parishes in the southern climates, many do not do Catholics Returning Home during the fall because of the heat. No sense in trying to fish when the fish aren't there and biting!

## Getting the word out

The publicity and outreach are critical. Thus, see the next chapter on publicity, which includes samples along with all the details.

## Chapter 4

# Publicity for Outreach

## Publicity is key — The more the better

Publicity outreach is critical for the success of Catholics Returning Home. The number of people responding and attending relates directly to how well the publicity gets out. I've written up all the publicity that you need for Catholics Returning Home. See the detailed write-ups listed in this chapter. They are a time saver so that you don't need to re-invent the wheel. They've been used everywhere and they work like a charm. However, over time, you can author additional materials for variety.

The publicity for the Catholics Returning Home series should begin six weeks before the sessions start up and continue until the week of the series' first week. For the Christmas series, the publicity should begin after Thanksgiving; for the Easter series, the publicity kicks off at the beginning of Lent; and for the Fall series, publicity starts near the end of July.

The publicity should include: bulletin articles, outdoor signs and banners, newspaper notices and releases (if possible), flyers, brochures, paid ads in the newspapers, radio, and TV (if budget permits), electronic media, Prayers of the Faithful, and announcements before the Christmas and Easter Masses and before the beginning of the Fall series. If the parish has a website, or Facebook page, a write-up or page for Catholics Returning Home should be included along with a contact name, email address, and/or phone number. You can't overdo publicity! Many parishes say they notice an increase in attendance just by running the publicity. Some people return to the Church after seeing the publicity without calling or attending a Catholics Returning Home series.

## Putting the nets out to catch fish

The bulletin articles, inserts, and announcements are aimed at the congregation, to encourage them to invite their non-practicing friends, family, and acquaintances and to bring them to the six-week series. I also talk before all the Masses during Lent, encouraging them to pray for their non-practicing brethren and to give them copies of the outreach publicity and help them return. Sometimes people show up at the six-week series with flyers and handouts and say their neighbor or friend handed them the paperwork and said, "Take this, you need it." Not the most polished, but it did the job! All this publicity works so well at getting the attention of those who are away. It's miraculous how effective it is. Sometimes people say they were away a lifetime and then they started seeing all the signs and banners over and over, and the Lord touched their hearts and prompted them to act. One woman who was away thirty-two years said, after driving by the signs for a while, one morning she was making coffee, looking out her kitchen window, and she heard the Lord telling her it's time to get back to church…so she attended the six-week series and reconciled and renewed her relationship with the Lord and the Church. Yet another changed and transformed life through the Lord's grace!

It's important to stop the outreach publicity when the new series begins, or else you'll continue to get new people coming throughout the series. It's best that new people start at the beginning and attend both the first and second session, because that's where the storytelling, venting, and sharing occurs. However, if people get the courage to come forward and ask to attend, I don't like to make them wait for months until the next series starts. Therefore, I tell them they are welcome to join the group. I still have them complete the anonymous questionnaire (see page 97) to allow them to "catch up" with the rest of the group by expressing their feelings.

You should put an article in the bulletin to inform the congregation of the results of the series. It's important to provide the congregation with feedback, so they will continue their involvement and participation in outreach efforts and in welcoming returnees to the community. Some parishes have decided to keep the Catholics Returning Home publicity out permanently. If people come between the sessions, they work with them one-on-one until the next six-week series starts.

## Let your light shine

The outdoor signs and banners are critical. For small to medium-sized signs and banners less than 3 feet by 5 feet, it's best to stick with the simple wording I've designed, which is "Catholics Returning Home – Begins Soon – call xxx-xxxx." We designed a large banner/billboard (see page 60), when you have more space to work with. Some parishes have huge banners on their grounds that are visible from their busy roads. Others use the large highway billboards, because the rates are really cheap when vacant.

I have my phone number all over the place, on signs, newspapers, and flyers, and I've never received a crank phone call. If you don't want to put someone's phone number on the sign, you can use the parish number. But if you do this, you must make sure that the parish is prepared to take the calls. They should get the names and phone numbers of returnees and pass that information on to the team members. And, they should also give the team members' names and phone numbers to the callers. When the team members take the initial calls, it's important that they're friendly, accepting, and welcoming. They should find out how the returnee found out about the series, and get the person's name and phone number, and explain to them the basics of the program.

At Christmas and Easter Masses, all the priests should say a few words of welcome to returning Catholics and invite them to the upcoming sessions. It's magic if it comes out of the priests' mouths. Many returnees have said they just happened to attend Mass at Christmas or Easter, after being away for many years and seeing the signs and banners. When Father welcomed back the returning Catholics, they just knew it was meant for them. It's critical that the priests are given a write-up of what they're supposed to talk about and when. Also, a Catholics Returning Home team member could talk before the Masses and invite any returning Catholics to the series.

## Outdoor signs and banners on parish grounds and/or parishioners' homes and businesses

The signs and banners work great everywhere. They especially work well as yard signs and on chain-link fences on the parish grounds and Catholic cemeteries. Deacon John Rex, clergy representative for Catholics Returning Home, is based in the Archdiocese of Chicago. His day job is running a printing business called Lighthouse Printing. He has taken my write-ups for the signs, brochures, and flyers and used his graphics design skills to make them look beautiful as well as functional. See the examples within this chapter. You can get all your publicity materials locally, but you should follow our wording and set-up design, for maximum effectiveness. Otherwise, John has all the Catholics Returning Home publicity and advertising materials available for purchase at his printing business. Check out his website at https://lighthouseprinting.net/catholics-returning-home/ to see samples. You can get a camera-ready copy of the black and white CRH logo by contacting Sally or Deacon John, so that you can include them in all the publicity. In addition, you can download a Word document from John's website that contains all the forms and publicity materials, so you don't have to re-type everything.

Wording for outdoor signs and banners for small to medium sizes less than 3 feet by 5 feet:

Catholics Returning Home

Begins Soon

Call: xxx-xxx-xxxx

Optional: insert parish name

Here are samples of Deacon Rex's creations:

**"Catholics Returning Home"**

— Begins Soon —

**Call 708-479-7777**

St. Mary's of Mokena

Large banner/billboard:

# An Invitation to Non-Practicing Catholics:

CATHOLICS RETURNING HOME

Join us for an update series

PH: **800-123-4567**

# Wording for announcements:

<Insert parish name> Announcements and Prayers of the Faithful

We are asking each of you to make a special effort to ask any of your non-practicing friends, relatives, or acquaintances to attend our **Catholics Returning Home** series beginning < insert date, meeting location >. See bulletin announcement for more information.

We are asking each of you to make a special effort to ask any of your non-practicing friends, relatives, or acquaintances to join us for < select Lenten / Holy Week / Easter / Advent / Christmas > services. We invite them to attend our **Catholics Returning Home** series beginning < insert date, time, location >. See the bulletin announcement.

Our parish family is delighted that those of you who do not worship regularly with us chose to be with us for this < series Lenten / Holy Week / Advent Sunday / Christmas Celebration >. Please note the special announcement in the bulletin for the series entitled **Catholics Returning Home** which is for people who are away from the Church.

We welcome returning Catholics who are here to worship with us today. We have a special program for non-practicing Catholics who may be considering a return to the Church. This program begins < insert start date >. For more information, see details in the bulletin.

### Announcement by Presider Before or After Mass or During Homily

For those who have been away from the Church for whatever reason, we're delighted that you are here. We invite you to attend a special series called **Catholics Returning Home**, beginning < insert start date >. Please see the bulletin for details.

### Prayers of the Faithful

For all those who have drifted away from the Church, that we may be signs of the Lord's love and care for them.

That all who are separated from the Church may come to possess the great joy of knowing God's compassionate love and acceptance.

That those returning to the Church to celebrate with us during this < select Lenten / Easter / Advent / Christmas > season may be blessed with a renewal of faith and a closer walk with the Lord.

That those who are troubled and separated may find peace in the Sacrament of Reconciliation at our parish celebrations during this holy season.

For those who have left the Church, that the Lord's compassionate love will lead them back.

For those who accepted our invitation to return home to the Church, that they may be blessed with a renewal of faith and a closer walk with the Lord.

# Wording for Bulletin Articles

### CATHOLICS RETURNING HOME

Do you know someone who has left the Church? Most of us do not have to look very far to find non-practicing Catholics in our circle of family and friends. Many of us are concerned about these loved ones; however, we don't know how to help them. Obviously, most of them are searching, but how can we help them find their way home?

As baptized, practicing Catholics we have a precious gift of faith and love from the Lord that needs to be shared with our non-practicing brothers and sisters. First, we need to pray for them. Secondly, we need to extend a personal invitation to them to come home to the Catholic Church. Most non-practicing Catholics are waiting for an invitation to return. Many mistakenly think they are excommunicated and are not welcome to return for a variety of reasons.

Many non-practicing Catholics carry a tremendous amount of guilt and misinformation about the Church, so they are afraid of approaching the Church for fear of being rejected. You can make a tremendous difference in someone's life, simply by reaching out to them and telling them that we miss them and would like for them to come back home to our Church family.

Here at < insert parish name >, we have a special program to help non-practicing Catholics return to the Church called **Catholics Returning Home**. The next series begins < insert start date, place, and time >. Please pass this article on to anyone who might be interested. For more information, call < insert **Catholics Returning Home** coordinator's name, phone number, and/or email >.

### Catholics Returning Home

< insert parish name > will offer a six-week series entitled **Catholics Returning Home** beginning < insert start date, time, and place >. The sessions are for non-practicing Catholics who are seeking answers to questions about returning to the Church. If you know someone who has left the Church, please invite them to join us. For more information, call < insert **Catholics Returning Home** coordinator's name, phone number, and/or email >.

### Have You Drifted Away from the Church?

Are you angry with the Church or God? Please give us a chance to listen to and address your concerns. Join us for our informal weekly sessions beginning < insert start date, place, and time >. The meetings will be facilitated by former non-practicing Catholics who you may find share many of your feelings. In the meantime, if you have any questions, please call < insert **Catholics Returning Home** coordinator's name, phone number, and/or email >.

### An Invitation to Non-Practicing Catholics

The Church has changed and you may not know it! Has it been a while since you've been to Church??? Are you mad at the Church or at God? Please give us, and yourself another chance. Join us for informal sessions for non-practicing Catholics. We would like to know your feelings and try to address your questions.

The meetings will be held in < insert time and place > on six consecutive < day > evenings beginning < insert start date >. If you have any questions in the meantime, please call < insert **Catholics Returning Home** coordinator' s name, phone number, and/or email >.

### GET RID OF THOSE NEGATIVE FEELINGS!!

Have you been hurt or angered by the Church? There are others who may share many of your feelings. Please give the Church and yourself another chance by joining us at six weekly sessions on < insert day > evenings at < insert time and place > beginning < insert start date >. Former non-practicing Catholics will share their stories and listen to your feelings and concerns. There is no obligation, and perhaps some of your questions will be answered. For more information, please call < insert **Catholics Returning Home** coordinator's name, phone number, and/ or email >.

### AN INVITATION FOR NON-PRACTICING CATHOLICS

If you are a Catholic who has been away from the Church for a while, this invitation is for you. No matter how long you have been away and no matter what reason, we invite you to consider renewing your relationship with the Catholic Church. Please join us for informal listening sessions and an update of the Catholic faith facilitated by former non-practicing Catholics. No strings attached!

< Insert place > on six consecutive < insert day > evenings at < insert time > beginning < insert start date >. For more information, call < insert **Catholics Returning Home** coordinator's name, phone number, and/or email >.

## CATHOLICS RETURNING HOME

We are happy to report that we have had numerous calls from people seeking answers to questions about returning to the Catholic Church. Many have been attending our meetings over the last several months on < insert day > evenings at < insert time and place >. These are people of all ages who have been away from the Church. Our next series begins < insert day, start date, time, and place >. We would like to invite anyone who is interested to join us. Please call < insert **Catholics Returning Home** coordinator's name, phone number, and/or email > for more information.

## CATHOLICS RETURNING HOME

Have you been away from the Church for a while? Have you ever thought about returning? If so, we would like to welcome you back to < insert parish name >. We have a special ministry just for people like you who have been away from the Church. Please join us for a six-week series that begins < insert day, date, place and time >. We would like to address your questions and make you feel at home once more in the Catholic Church. For more information, please call < insert **Catholics Returning Home** coordinator' s name, phone number, and/or email >.

CATHOLICS
RETURNING
HOME

### CATHOLICS RETURNING HOME

- Were you raised Catholic but do not come or seldom come to Church anymore?
- Are you a Catholic who now feels separated from your Church?
- Would you like to know more about the Catholic Church as it is today?
- Would you like to feel at home in the Catholic Church again?

No matter how long you have been away and no matter what reason, we invite you to consider renewing your relationship with the Catholic Church.

Date: < insert start day and date >

Time: < insert time >

Place: < insert parish name and place >

For more information, call < insert **Catholics Returning Home** coordinator's name, phone number, and/ or email >.

## CATHOLICS RETURNING HOME

*An Invitation for Non-Practicing Catholics*

- Were you raised Catholic but do not come or seldom come to Church anymore?
- Are you a Catholic who now feels separated from the Church?
- Would you like to know more about the Catholic Church as it is today?
- Would you like to feel at home in the Catholic Church again?

No matter how long you have been away and no matter what reason, we invite you to consider renewing your relationship with the Catholic Church. Please join us for informal listening sessions and an update of the Catholic faith. The sessions are held at < insert start day, date, time, and place >. For more information, call < insert **Catholics Returning Home** coordinator's name, phone number, and/or email >.

CATHOLICS
RETURNING
HOME

CATHOLICS RETURNING HOME
< Weekday, time, and meeting location >

**Schedule**

| | |
|---|---|
| \<insert start date\> | Welcome |
| | Overview of series |
| | Sharing by team and attendees |
| \<insert session date\> | Video Stories of Faith from Catholics |
| | Returning Home |
| | Discussion and sharing |
| \<insert session date\> | The Church Today: Changes Since Vatican II |
| | Explanation of major changes |
| | (Mass in English, involvement, Bible study) |
| \<insert session date\> | Walk-through of the Mass |
| | (along with explanation and discussion) |
| \<insert session date\> | Tips on Sinning |
| | Explanation of the Sacrament of |
| | Reconciliation (Confession) |
| \<insert session date\> | The Creed: What Catholics Believe, |
| | discussion |

**CATHOLICS RETURNING HOME**
AN OPEN DOOR FOR RETURNING CATHOLICS
< insert parish names >
Welcome

- Were you raised Catholic but do not come or seldom come to Church anymore?
- Are you a Catholic who now feels separated from the Church?
- Would you like to know more about the Catholic Church as it is today?
- Would you like to feel at home in the Catholic Church again?

No matter how long you have been away and no matter what reason, we invite you to consider renewing your relationship with the Catholic Church.

Date: < insert start date >
Time: < insert start time >
Place: < insert place >

Sponsored by the < insert area name > Catholic Parishes

The following tri-fold brochure is designed to have prospective sponsors pay for the printing. The back page, which shows up blank on the following example, is for sponsor advertising. You can check with various church organizations and/or local businesses who might be interested in paying for the brochure to support the CRH ministry. Interested businesses might be the current bulletin advertisers. They in turn will benefit from the advertising, since the brochures should be distributed everywhere. Some parishes hand out these flyers and brochures at their local commuter train stations as people are coming and going to work.

The tri-fold brochure example shows the inside and outside pages. The blank back page is for sponsor ads.

## Directions

```
┌─────────────────────┐
│                     │
│                     │
│                     │
│     Map and         │
│     Directions      │
│     Here            │
│                     │
│                     │
│                     │
└─────────────────────┘
```

All sessions will be held at:
**Your Church Name**
**Address**
**Phone**

Please pass this on to anyone who might be interested! Everyone is welcome, no matter where they are from.

## Catholics Returning Home Schedule

**Spring 2007**

April 11    Welcome. "Why Am I Here?"

April 18    Video - Sharing Stories of Faith

April 25    The Church Today: Changes Since Vatican II

May 2    Explanation of the Mass

May 9    Explanation of Reconciliation

May 6    The Creed: What Catholics Believe

Catholics Returning Home sessions are offered as a six-week series. Sessions are from (time & place). The sessions are structured in a support-group format. Therefore, participants are free to attend as many or as few sessions as they wish.

## You're Invited...

If you are a **CATHOLIC** who has been **AWAY** from the **CHURCH** for a while, this **INVITATION** is for **YOU!** Our Faith Community misses you and is incomplete without you!

*No matter how long you have been away or for whatever reason, we invite you to* **CONSIDER** *renewing your relationship with the Catholic Church.*

*Please join us for informal listening sessions and an update of the Catholic faith facilitated by former non-practicing Catholics. The sessions are conducted in a support-group format.*

*Everyone is* WELCOME, *no matter where they are from!*

Catholics Returning Home

*An Invitation To Non-Practicing Catholics*

We WELCOME You Home!

Church Name
Address
Phone

Website

**Parable of the Lost Sheep:**

Jesus, the Good Shepherd, leaves the 99 sheep to seek the one that is lost. And, when he finds it, he brings it home, and calls everyone in heaven to rejoice more over the one repentant sinner than over the 99 who have no need of repentance.

Gospel of St. Luke 15:3-7

"Catholics Returning Home"
An Open Door For Returning Catholics

(your parish name here)

Welcome . . .

- Were you raised Catholic but do not come or seldom come to Church anymore?
- Are you a Catholic who now feels separated from the church?
- Would you like to know more about the Catholic church as it is
- today? Would you like to feel at home in the Catholic Church again?

No matter how long you have been away and no matter what reason, we invite you to consider renewing your relationship with the Catholic Church.

Date:   (insert  date)
Time:   (insert  time)
Place:   (insert place)

# Catholics Returning Home
## Welcome!
## (Church Name Here)
## Welcomes you
## home!

If you are a Catholic who has been away from the Church for awhile, this invitation is for you. Our faith community misses you and is incomplete without you. No matter how long you have been away, and for whatever reason, we invite you to consider renewing your relationship with the Catholic Church.

Please join us for informal listening sessions and an update of the Catholic faith facilitated by former non-practicing Catholics. The sessions are conducted in a support-group format. Everyone is welcome, no matter where they are from.

(Church Name) will conduct this ongoing series on six consecutive (day) evenings at (time)
beginning (date). For more details call (phone number).

# CATHOLICS RETURNING HOME

## An Invitation for Non-Practicing Catholics

- Were you raised Catholic but do not come or seldom come to Church anymore?
- Are you a Catholic who now feels separated from the church?
- Would you like to know more about the Catholic church as it is today?
- Would you like to feel at home in the Catholic Church again?

No matter how long you have been away and no matter what reason, we invite you to consider renewing your relationship with the Catholic Church. Please join us for informal listening sessions and an update of the Catholic faith. The sessions are held at (insert start day, date, time, and place). For more information, call (insert Catholics Returning Home coordinator's name and phone number).

### Catholics Returning Home
### 2006 Schedule

| | |
|---|---|
| (Insert Start Date) | Welcome<br>Overview of Series<br>Sharing by team and attendees |
| (Insert Session Date) | Video "Stories of Faith from Catholics Returning Home"<br>Discussion and sharing |
| (Insert Session Date) | The Church Today: Changes since Vatican II<br>Explanation of major changes<br>(Mass in English, Involvement, Bible Study) |
| (Insert Session Date) | Walk through of the Mass<br>(along with explanation and historical overview) |
| (Insert Session Date) | Tips on Sinning -<br>Explanation of the Sacrament of Reconciliation (Confession) |
| (Insert Session Date) | The Creed: What Catholics Believe |

## Newspaper Press Release

Because newspapers are very restrictive on allowing free publicity, it's best to offer them a longer and shorter version of the news release. They can then choose the one that fits their available space without their having to edit it. In addition, I add a short sentence on the release telling them not to edit it because I've never been happy with their shortened versions, which were almost unrecognizable.

### CATHOLICS RETURNING HOME

< insert parish name, address > will conduct an ongoing series called **Catholics Returning Home** on six consecutive < insert day of the week > evenings @ < insert start time and place > beginning < insert start date >. These sessions are for non-practicing Catholics who are seeking answers to questions about returning to the Church. There will be informal sharing and an update of the Catholic faith. For more details, call < insert **Catholics Returning Home** coordinator's name, phone number, and/or email>.

### CATHOLICS RETURNING HOME

Non-practicing Catholics are invited to informal listening sessions and an update of the Catholic faith. This six-week series begins < insert start date and time > at < insert parish name and city >. For details, call < insert **Catholics Returning Home** coordinator's name, phone number, and/or email >.

Note: Please do not edit the above articles!!

## Newspaper/Radio/TV Publicity

Some newspapers, TV, and radio stations still allow some free public service notices. They all have different requirements and forms. You'll have to research the possibilities in your area. I recommend making a list of the newspapers, TV, and radio station names and contact information, including any requirements for special forms and timing. These types of listings are especially useful during ministerial turnover, for continuity.

# Chapter 5

## Details of Sessions 1 and 2

## Session #1

### CHECKLIST FOR SESSIONS 1-6

- The same two to five team members for the six-week series, wearing name tags identifying them as team members
- A comfortable, easy to find meeting room with table and chairs
- A candle and lighter
- A box of tissues
- Name tags for attendees
- A listing of team members, including phone numbers
- Optional: You can include the Mass times and locations where team members attend, so that returnees can join them
- Copies of the Prayer of Thomas Merton

- Schedule for Catholics Returning Home six-week series, showing topics by week (see bulletin insert on page 69)
- Copies of *Handbook for Catholics* or similar booklet
- Copies of parish bulletins and any other information about parish activities
- Optional: Copies of *Returning Home to Your Catholic Faith*
- Optional: Beverages, bottled water, and snacks
- Optional: Invite leaders from the divorced/remarriage and bereavement ministries to attend the meeting and introduce themselves to the returnees
- Optional: Copies of *YouCat,* the Youth Catechism

### CHECKLIST FOR SESSION #1 ONLY

- Signs and greeters outside, directing people how to find the meeting room
- Blank, anonymous questionnaires
- Sign-in sheet
- Optional: Invite the pastor or associate to stop by and introduce himself and welcome attendees back to the Church

# Welcome and Completion of Anonymous Questionnaires

The Holy Spirit is the inspiration and guide for Catholics Returning Home ministry. Anyone called to this ministry either as a team member or a returnee is called by the Holy Spirit. By including petitions for returning Catholics in the Prayers of the Faithful during Mass, we're asking for the grace and guidance of the Holy Spirit. Throughout the preparation for meetings and in the meetings themselves, all the team members should pray for the Spirit's guidance and help. In addition, many parishes ask any surrounding religious communities and monasteries for prayer before and throughout the series. Some Catholics Returning Home teams meet fifteen minutes before the sessions and pray to the Holy Spirit for guidance throughout the evening.

The first session is the most important of the six sessions because it sets the tone for the rest of the series. If people get the nerve up to come to the first session and have a good experience, they will most likely continue.

Priests shouldn't attend the first or second sessions because some returnees are afraid of priests and some get angrier when priests are there. If the pastor or associate is available, he can stop in for five minutes to greet the returnees and welcome them back and then he leaves.

The room should be easy to find and comfortable. It's better to have a smaller, cozier room than a big open gym or parish hall. There should be outdoor and indoor signs pointing out how to find the meeting room. Greeters should be outside telling people where the room is and helping them as needed. I like to have a candle burning on the table. The team members should have name tags identifying them as part of the team. I prefer having a table with chairs around it, instead of just chairs because the group will be writing.

The meeting should run for an hour and a half. For the first session, I start about five to ten minutes late to allow late arrivers time to get there. I do make it a point to end on time, telling the attendees that we stick with the schedule for starting and quitting in order to respect their commitments. I tell them that the team will stay after the meeting to talk with them should any returnees desire to do so.

The team members should be prepared to talk a bit about themselves. Those who have been away from the Church and returned should briefly share some of those experiences as they initially identify themselves as team members when introduced to the group. Those team members who have never left the Church should also share their experiences in the same way. It doesn't matter that they haven't left and come back; they should share why they have stayed, or if they have struggled. When the team members talk, it should appear to be natural and relaxed and not rehearsed and "canned." Never say, "I've been asked to share…," because it somewhat invalidates whatever is shared and sounds contrived and staged.

As people enter the room, the team members should greet them and make small talk before the meeting begins. You can give the early arrivers their paperwork right away so they can look through the information and get a head start, or you can wait until everyone is seated before handing out the paperwork.

The agenda should be strictly followed for the first meeting in order to control and manage the meeting content. However, it works best if the meeting flow looks seamless rather than referring constantly to an agenda. Returnees seem to feel more comfortable and open up more, if the meeting is firmly controlled but doesn't look stiff and contrived. This can be a delicate balance. Without an agenda, it's almost impossible to maintain control and keep the meeting positive when there are some really angry attendees. I don't break the returnees into smaller groups, even if the group is large because it's too easy to lose control. The likelihood of angry people taking over a smaller group is too high in the small-group format to take the risk.

The agenda should be strictly followed, even if some returnees who aren't particularly angry want to veer off in various directions. One such example is if a few insist on talking about divorce and annulment issues. No matter how adamant and forceful they are, it's best to say you're not an expert in those areas and you will be happy to route them to the particular person in the parish that handles that issue. You can even offer to talk with them after the session that night, but insist that right now the group is going to continue with what is on the agenda for the evening. It doesn't really matter what the issue is that someone wants to deviate toward — never abandon the agenda, because you will lose most of the rest of the group and it will make the meeting look disorganized and unprepared. The people that want to veer off in different directions are primarily served by working through the agenda items as well. It's much better to kindly and calmly address their concerns with a few words, tell them you're happy to talk with them after the session that night, and/or put them in touch with someone in the parish, but right now — tonight — the group will be sticking to the agenda.

A critical exercise in the first week is working through the anonymous questionnaire (see page 97). It is an excellent spiritual and psychological tool. The questions are: 1) I am here because, 2) My hopes/expectations in being here are, 3) My fears/apprehensions about being here are, 4) My feelings about the Church are, 5) My feelings about God at this time are, 6) The questions/issues I most want answered in these sessions are, plus a section for other comments.

Each of the questions is designed to keep the returnees on track and elicit out of them the real purpose they are there, which is because the Lord has been gently and lovingly working in their hearts and they have answered his call by coming forward after being a long way off. The questions cut through to the heart of the matter. By responding to this questionnaire, each of them loses their defenses, bluster, and smoke screens, and gets right on point about their relationship with God and the Church. Over time from one group to another, the responses are almost identical with the same words, expressions, and sentiments. Overwhelmingly, they have a deep spiritual hunger and emptiness that they desperately want to alleviate by returning home to their Catholic faith. They usually have positive feelings about God and mixed feelings about the Church. Their fears are that they won't be accepted or there isn't a place for them. The questions they have are 99.9% related to their status in the Church as to whether or not they will be accepted. And, if they do have any valid questions, they are usually really simple grade-school level that are easily answered by the team. However, occasionally, they can ask a question or two that may be a bit more complex. In that case, it's pretty simple to look it up in the Catechism and you can even show them how to do so. The youth Catechism is particularly helpful for the returnees because it is at a beginner's level and has a terrific index of topics that they can peruse. Part of the responsibility of growing and maturing in our Catholic faith is to begin the life long journey of discovery and learning, and they might as well get used to the process upfront.

The anonymous questionnaire also allows them to vent on paper their anger and frustrations about the Church in a structured and controlled manner. The team members should also complete the questionnaires because this tends to make the returnees feel more comfortable. During the discussion, the team members should be talking about their responses right along with the returnees. This helps to blur any distinctions of "we-they" between the team members and the returnees, which seems to help them shed any defenses and hostility.

Never have team members obviously observe, monitor, or watch the returnees. Most of the returnees are walking on eggshells, skittish, and nervous. To have team members "watching" them, "sizing them up," and evaluating them is entirely too intimidating and threatening for most returnees to handle. Some might leave almost immediately, if they sense they're being studied like insects under a microscope. The team members should learn to blend in with the returnees, listening to them and trying to make them feel comfortable and at ease.

## Agenda: Management Tool to Control the Meeting

### 1. Introduction and Prayer

The leader introduces him/herself and welcomes all attendees. Next, the leader says he/she's going to read the Prayer of Thomas Merton, and if they care to, the group can join in and read along or, if they're not comfortable doing so, they can just listen. The Prayer of Thomas Merton follows:

> My Lord God, I have no idea where I am going. I do not see the road ahead of me. I cannot know for certain where it will end. Nor do I really know myself, and the fact that I think that I am following Your will, does not mean that I am actually doing so.
>
> But I believe that the desire to please You does — in fact — please You. And I hope that I have that desire in all that I am doing. I hope that I will never do anything apart from that desire.
>
> And I know that if I do this, You will lead me by the right road though I may know nothing about it. Therefore, will I trust You always though I may seem to be lost and in the shadow of death. I will not fear, for You are ever with me, and You will never leave me to face my perils alone.

After reading the prayer, explain that Thomas Merton was a modern-day Trappist monk who was involved in ecumenism with Eastern religions and that he died in the 1960s. He's written a number of books and is a popular author. I always mention how I feel his prayer speaks to all of us, but especially returning Catholics, because it describes how the Lord is with each of us, guiding us, even when we're not aware of his presence.

I tell them that just as the Prayer of Thomas Merton indicates, everyone who is present at the meeting has been brought here by the Holy Spirit. And as we hear some of the stories from those present, the guidance of the Holy Spirit will be confirmed when we see all of the different paths that everyone travelled to be here. In the same way Jesus the Good Shepherd left the ninety-nine sheep to seek out the one who was lost, Jesus has sought out every one of them and brought them here. We know it took a lot of courage for them to call and to walk in the door, and we're glad they're here.

Explain to the group that in order to respect the privacy of all who are present, everyone should regard the content and conversation of the meeting as confidential and not to be shared outside the group. Many people who have been away from the Church have a church story and beneath it a big bundle of hurts. Talking through our church stories or faith journeys frequently helps us to deal with other issues in our lives. But, we'll only be working with the church story because we're not counselors or therapists.

I tell the group that Catholics Returning Home was started because the Church wants those who have drifted away to return. Many people might think they're not welcome or excommunicated, but in truth they're all invited to return. All the Church rules and regulations are still in place, and if some people have questions about divorce and remarriage, they can work through those concerns with our parish staff who handle such issues. Though certain issues and obstacles may seem overwhelming, there is nothing a returnee can't work through with the help of the Lord.

I then ask the team members to introduce themselves. They should each take a minute or two and say their names, welcome those who have returned, mention if they themselves have been away and returned (or if not, mention why they choose to be a part of the Church and note some of the struggles they've had). Perhaps team members will want to mention what they do for a living and/or in what other parish activities they participate.

After introduction of the team members, the team leader explains that the sessions are informal and that attendees will have a chance to ask questions and learn about what the Church is like today throughout the coming sessions. Hand out the list of team members' names, phone numbers, and emails. Encourage the returnees to call or email when they have questions or concerns.

Hand out the schedule of what will be covered over the next six weeks (see page 69). Tell the returnees they have no obligation to attend each session, but it will help their progress if they do commit to regular attendance. If they do miss a session, they're more than welcome to attend the next series and repeat any or all of the sessions. Some people have attended off and on for years, which is fine. Because there are always new people in the group, the sessions are always somewhat different.

Hand out the sign-in sheet (see page 98) for them to fill out their names, towns, emails, and phone numbers. Explain that they are under no obligation to sign in. It's

really important for the team to know how each returnee found out about the sessions, so that the team can
improve its outreach publicity. Also, having the names,
emails, and phone numbers of the group members helps
the team communicate with the returnees in case a meeting changes. You can include the Mass times and locations where the team members attend so that the returnees can join them if they like. The returnees will not be
officially registered with the parish at this time. If they
want to register with the parish, they will need to contact
the parish office.

Distribute any parish bulletins, booklets, and pamphlets that pertain to parish activities and scheduled services. Tell them about the *Handbook for Catholics* (or a
similar guide to Catholic beliefs, practices, prayers, and
integration of the Faith into one's daily life), *YouCat*, and
*Returning Home to Your Catholic Faith*. Some parishes
give the booklets away, others ask for a token donation to
offset the costs. I also encourage returnees to get a Bible
and read the Psalms and the Gospels, especially chapter
15 of the Gospel of Luke, which contains the parables of
Divine Mercy. I tell them that when I started reading the
Bible, I got a children's Bible for children of all ages because it gave me a place to start. A good children's Bible
has all the stories that a regular Bible does, and it's ref-
erenced to a regular Bible so that the reader can start at
a level where they're able to understand, and later can
move on to a more technical level.

Hand out the open-ended anonymous questionnaire
(see page 97) along with the pens/pencils and allow the
group ten minutes or so to complete them. Inform the

group that the questionnaires are anonymous — they shouldn't put their names on them. Mention that expressing their feelings on paper is a healing step, and many returning Catholics have a lot of questions, concerns, and feelings of guilt. Let the returnees know that the group will discuss the questionnaire that night and collect their questionnaires before they leave so the team can read them.

### 2. COMPLETING THE QUESTIONNAIRE

After ten minutes or so, when it looks like most are finished completing the questionnaire, the leader informs the returnees that the group is going to talk about the responses given on the questionnaires. Assure the returnees that they do not have to share their comments if they do not want to, because there are always plenty in the group who want to talk and share. The leader starts out with the first question and says, "I am here because..." and explains a bit why he/she is here. Next, each of the team members answer the same question. At this point, the leader and team members can share more about themselves, for example, how they came to be a part of this ministry.

Next, the team leader asks if anyone else would like to share their response to question #1. Again, assure the group that no one should feel put on the spot. The leader can start going around the room in order, passing over the team, because they have already responded. For those returnees that are hesitant, pass them by, and go on to the next returnee. Usually, some of the returnees want to share. Let each one answer the question. Notice that we are channeling and managing the discussion down a path where we are eliciting certain information from the returnees. Some of the more angry returnees that might be there may try to jump in and dominate the discussion, ranting and raving on unrelated topics. The team leader has to listen very carefully, and allow some venting, but if a returnee gets too far off the path, the team leader will have to make a judgment and gently but firmly return the discussion to the matter at hand, which is answering question #1: I'm here because. Some strategies are to thank the returnee for sharing and then say, "We're going to get back to the discussion and let some others have a chance to participate." If someone tries to interrupt or change the topic, the team leader can say, "No, we're not talking about that topic right now. See me later if you like, but right now, we're going to talk about this topic."

Give everyone a chance to talk about question #1. Then repeat the procedure for question #2. Again, first let the team leader and each of the team members answer the question. Then, go around the room and ask each and every one of the returnees to share their response to question #2. Repeat the same procedure for all of the questions.

### 3. Optional: Profile Sharing

Instead of discussing the entire anonymous questionnaire in #2 above, you can plan to break off that discussion and have one of the team members share their story of being away and returning for about 10-15 minutes. Some of the stories are so touching and moving that they are very effective in helping the returnees know they are among peers, feel comfortable, and bond with the group. The team member who shares should be able to tell their story in a relaxed, natural manner without notes. Don't say, "I've been asked to..." Instead, be able to simply talk about your experiences without looking like it's "canned" or rehearsed. Returnees seem to open up more if the discussion and sharing is free flowing and natural.

### 4. End the session on time!

The leader should tell the group that the session is ending out of respect for everyone's time and commitments. If anyone wants to stay afterward, the team will remain for a while. Anyone who needs to leave can leave now or after the closing prayer. If anyone wants to join in the closing prayer, they're welcome to do so.

### 5. Closing Prayer

If the meeting room is in or near the church, I prefer to gather around the altar for the closing prayer. Gathering and praying around the altar might at first seem rather inappropriate for returnees; however, it has a profoundly positive impact on them. They can't believe they're worthy enough to be invited to gather around the altar. You can see the peace and tranquility on their faces at being gathered and included in such a prayer. If the meeting room isn't in or near the church, then just gather around the table in the meeting room. Once everyone is gathering around either the altar or the table, ask all who care to participate to join hands and pray the Our Father together.

After praying the Our Father, the team should remain for a while to answer questions and talk with those returnees who have specific questions and concerns. Be sure and collect their completed anonymous question-naires before they leave.

### 6. FOLLOW-UP

After the first meeting and throughout the six-week series, the team leader and members of the team should call all of the attendees and offer to answer any questions they may have. The returnees really appreciate the indi-vidual attention, and some people seem to be more com-fortable talking individually than in a group. These in-dividual conversations are where the returnees have the opportunity to ask open-ended questions and seek help with their personal situations.

# Session #2
# Sharing Stories of Faith

Items to have on hand and things to do before the session starts:
- Checklist for Sessions 1-6 from Chapter 5, Session #1

### CHECKLIST FOR SESSION 2 ONLY:
- Have video *Stories of Faith from Catholics Returning Home* (see page 129)
- Have DVD and TV set up and ready to go
- Handouts on specific Catholic issues such as annul-ments, divorce/remarriage, and so on

During the first week, the focus is on the personal stories of the group and the related sharing and venting.

During the second week, the focus shifts from those stories within the small group to the Church at large. The video, *Stories of Faith from Catholics Returning Home*, works very well to make the transition. The transition allows the returnees to be listened to, affirmed for their experiences, and aided in letting go of past disappointments and hurts. By viewing the video and relating it to their own stories, they are able to acknowledge that others as well as themselves have been disappointed or hurt by the Church, that the Church is filled with imperfect human beings who make mistakes, and that it's time to move on and let go of past disappointments or hurts instead of staying stuck in anger or resentment. The discussion is managed by having the returnees relate their stories to those seen in the video. In this way, they're being guided along a specific path of discussion, so they don't go off on tangents.

The team welcomes the returnees back for the second week as they arrive. If there are new attendees, give them copies of the blank, anonymous questionnaire and have them complete it. Also give them copies of the team listing, schedule of the upcoming sessions, and any other paperwork and books that have already been given to the others.

The leader introduces him/herself and welcomes all the attendees including the newcomers. Next, the leader says he/she's going to read the Prayer of Thomas Merton (see page 99), inviting everyone to join in and read along.

Just as they did in the first session, the team members introduce themselves to the group. This is helpful for newcomers as well as those who were there the previous week in bonding with the team members.

The leader summarizes in general terms the anonymous questionnaires that were handed out at the previous session, which were collected and reviewed by the team. The leader mentions that many of the responses are very similar, showing that we're not alone in our search for the Lord and our way back to the Church. The leader should comment only on common themes within the questionnaires, such as the fact that everyone in the group is searching and trying to find their way home and their own place in the Church. The returnees should be informed that they are united in this journey with those in the Church who are involved in the same ongoing search — this is one of the comforts of being part of the Church. Answer any questions that can be easily summarized and addressed.

Next, the team leader introduces *Stories of Faith from Catholics Returning Home*. The most important parts of the video are the actual stories as told by the returnees. Tell the group they should pay close attention to these narratives and try to relate some part of their own life stories to them, because that's what the group will talk about next.

After viewing the video, the team leader makes a few comments about how the stories chronicled in the video relate to his/her own life story. Next, each team member relates the video to their lives. If any of the returnees get off track, firmly bring them back to the video and their own lives.

The discussion process of the first and second sessions allows returnees to vent and let go of any pent-up anger and hurt they hold toward the Church. One can see the change in the returnees each week as they become more comfortable and relaxed within the group and the Church.

Try to end the session on time, stopping the discussion around ten minutes early in order to have time for the closing prayer. Gather around the altar if possible, hold hands, and invite the group to pray the Our Father. All the team members should stay afterward to talk to any returnees that have issues or questions.

## SESSION #1

ANONYMOUS QUESTIONNAIRE          DATE: _____

1. I am here because:

_____

_____

2. My hopes/expectations in being here are:

_____

_____

3. My fears/apprehensions about being here are:

_____

_____

4. My feelings about the Church are:

_____

_____

5. My feelings about God at this time are:

_____

_____

6. The questions/issues I most want answered:

_____

_____

Other Comments:

_____

_____

_____

_____

SIGN-IN SHEET          WEEK #1          DATE: _____

| Name | City | Phone # / email | How did you find out about these sessions? |
|------|------|-----------------|---------------------------------------------|
| 1. | | | |
| 2. | | | |
| 3. | | | |
| 4. | | | |
| 5. | | | |
| 6. | | | |
| 7. | | | |
| 8. | | | |
| 9. | | | |
| 10. | | | |
| 11. | | | |
| 12. | | | |
| 13. | | | |
| 14. | | | |
| 15. | | | |
| 16. | | | |
| 17. | | | |
| 18. | | | |
| 19. | | | |
| 20. | | | |

**WEEK #1**

< insert parish name & address >

**TEAM**

< insert team members' name, phone #, email, Sunday Mass time, and church usually attended >

## Prayer of Thomas Merton

My Lord God, I have no idea where I am going. I do not see the road ahead of me. I cannot know for certain where it will end. Nor do I really know myself, and the fact that I think that I am following Your will, does not mean that I am actually doing so.

But I believe that the desire to please You does — in fact — please You. And I hope that I have that desire in all that I am doing. I hope that I will never do anything apart from that desire.

And I know that if I do this, You will lead me by the right road though I may know nothing about it. Therefore, will I trust You always though I may seem to be lost and in the shadow of death. I will not fear, for You are ever with me, and You will never leave me to face my perils alone.

## Chapter 6

# Details of Sessions 3-6

## Session #3
## The Church Today: Changes Since Vatican II

Items to have on hand and things to do before the session starts:

- Checklist for Sessions 1-6 from Chapter 5, Session #1

### CHECKLIST FOR SESSION 3 ONLY:

- Schedule a team member or other presenter to give the presentation, or
- Show a thirty-minute video on Vatican II
- Have DVD and TV set up and ready to go
- Handout on Pre- and Post-Vatican II (see page 121)

Some people ask me why do I have a session on Vatican II since it's ancient history. My response is that we are living in a post Vatican II Church that has been

profoundly shaped by the Second Council's pronounce-
ments and documents. Therefore, in order to understand
today's Church, we must start with a brief explanation
of the effects of the Second Council. The emphasis and
primary objective of this session is to focus on what is
going on in today's Church and describe some of the
activities in order to help the returnees feel they're welcome and can fit in. The references to Vatican II history
should be brief and meant as a reference point only, to
ground the returnees' understanding of today's Church.
This approach covers all returnees whether they've been
gone a few years or a lifetime. For those who are pre-Vatican II returnees, it helps them shift to the present. For
those who have been gone a short time and have only
heard stories about pre-Vatican II from their parents and
grandparents, it helps them understand and reconcile
those old stories with the updated information.

We need to give the returnees a top-level, big-picture
overview of what's going on in the Church today, along
with a brief history, while focusing on how they fit in and
that they're welcome and we want them back. Some parishes mistakenly get over complicated for this session by
trying to find the most educated, degreed expert in canon and/or civil law to give a presentation. Instead, what
is needed is simple and basic information presented in
a non-threatening friendly manner. This session should
be presented more like a coffee and donut welcoming/
hospitality, come and see gathering for new parishioners,
rather than a fact-based lecture. You must keep in mind
that the incoming returnees are just getting comfortable after their first two weeks of faith sharing and now

they're hungry for more, wondering what the Church is like, can they fit in, are they welcome, is there a place for me here? They don't need lots of heavy-duty theory, but instead kindness and acceptance.

The team leader reads the opening prayer composed by Thomas Merton (see page 99) and invites others to join along if they care to. A team member or presenter can give a brief explanation of the Second Vatican Council, saying it was the twenty-first Roman Catholic ecumenical council. Convened by Pope John XXIII, and conducted from 1962 to 1965, the Council's sixteen documents redefined the nature of the Church without changing any doctrine, gave bishops greater influence in Church affairs, and increased lay participation throughout the Church including the liturgy. Since Vatican II, the laity is extensively involved with planning, administration, and ministerial activities in dioceses and parishes everywhere. Some call the post-Vatican II Church "the age of the laity."

Even today, many of the changes are in flux and are being refined and fine-tuned to more accurately reflect the actual translation and intent. Implementation and practices vary from parish to parish and diocese to diocese. In some cases, some of the "old ways" are being brought back and re-integrated into Church life. People have left the Church because of too much change and not enough. Sometimes returnees are concerned about all the differences and disagreements from one parish or diocese to another. Assure them that the Lord is with his Church until the end of time, and he is protecting, leading, and guiding the way. Over time, he will make sure the Church goes in the direction that he has charted! In the meantime, we are so blessed in the Catholic Church to have so much variety, diversity, and choices, so that we can find the parish family that suits us, where we can feel welcome and at home.

Here is a listing of some changes you can talk about. Feel free to focus on any that fit your particular location or situation. For example, in some parishes where I've done CRH, the deacons rotated for this session. They would tell their personal stories and spend most of the time talking about the diaconate, explaining their differences from priests and their assignments.

Mass — We will discuss this more next week, but briefly: local vernacular language such as English, removal of communion rail, priest faces congregation, more congregational participation, larger variety of music including Protestant hymns, only an hour communion fast. In some dioceses, there are a few parishes that offer the Latin Mass.

Bible study groups — Breaking open the word groups, to study and reflect on the week's lectionary readings; many pre-Vatican II Catholics didn't study the Bible, it collected dust.

Lay involvement in liturgy — Eucharistic ministers, contemporary Mass, lay involvement in planning/organizing liturgy, laity decorating altar, lectors.

Lay ministry — Greater involvement of B.O.L.P.'s (basic, ordinary, laypersons), much more education and training for laity in pastoral ministry and theology, leadership roles in ministry, volunteer as well as paid, parish and arch/diocesan leadership for finance committee, greater involvement of women including girl altar serv-ers, each parishes' bulletin or website shows myriad of ministries by laity.

Diaconate (back to roots) — Deacons aren't married priests. They preside over: Baptism, weddings, funerals, and are involved in service to the community. Deacon couples are involved in formation, schooling, and min-istry for both.

Confession to Reconciliation — We will discuss this more in a few weeks, but briefly: life orientation vs. laun-dry list of sins, face to face vs. behind the screen, Fr. Ber-nard Haring's law of love — formerly, moral theologians were first trained as canon lawyers so their approach was law first. Fr. Bernard Haring in Vatican II changed moral theology toward an emphasis on law of love, thus Vatican II was called a civilization of love. The relationship be-tween God and people is of parent and child, primarily a relationship of love rather than a mere observance of law.

Hierarchal pyramid structure vs. community of faith-ful disciples, people of God, many parts, one body. Build-ing structures changed from rows and rows of pews that are back from the altar to circle around the altar to reflect that of a community of disciples rather than a hierarchy.

Pray, pay, and obey vs. discerning time, treasure, and talent. Formerly priests and sisters did everything. Now, very few sisters in parish ministry — they seem to be more involved in hospital or university administration. Most sisters no longer wear "habits."

More parish-based social outreach to food pantries and homeless shelters. More parish-based political in-volvement such as anti-war, anti-death penalty, and pro-life. Pre-Vatican II had the Dorothy Day Catholic Worker Movement for the poor and homeless mostly operating in larger cities and the US Bishops Catholic Action/Catholic Conference for pro-life work. After Vatican II, most parishes have established active pro-life ministries and a myriad of other social outreach ministries listed in the bulletins which are readily available to regular parishioners.

Ministry to divorced/remarried — Annulments not Catholic divorce. Now many support groups for divorced/remarried.

Ecumenism — Greater involvement with other denominations/churches. Pope John XXIII said the Church can now breathe with both lungs in describing the dialogue between Roman Catholic and Eastern Orthodox churches that had been separated for years.

If you don't have a presenter, just show a video on Vatican II. The main objective for the third week is to make the returnees comfortable in their Church today and feel that they fit in and belong.

At the conclusion of the session, call the group together for the closing prayer. Join hands and pray the Our Father. (Pray around the altar if possible.)

# Session #4
## The Mass and Optional Church Tour

- Checklist for Sessions 1-6 from Chapter 5, Session #1

### CHECKLIST FOR SESSION 4 ONLY:

- Schedule one or more team members or other presenters to give an explanation of the Mass, or
- Show a video on the Mass
- Have DVD and TV set up and ready to go

Begin with the Prayer of Thomas Merton (see page 99) for all who care to participate. Tell the returnees about the first Mass. At the end of Lent, we commemorate Holy Thursday, the Last Supper, and the first Holy Eucharist or the Sacrifice of the Mass instituted by Jesus the night before he was crucified and died on Good Friday. Holy Saturday night is the vigil of the Resurrection, and Easter Sunday is the celebration of Jesus' Resurrection.

> "Then, taking bread and giving thanks, he broke it and gave it to them saying: 'This is my body to be given for you. Do this as a remembrance of me.' He did the same with the cup after eating, saying as he did so: 'This cup is the new covenant in my blood, which will be shed for you'" (Luke 22:19-20).

In the Old Testament, the Jewish people sacrificed animals and offered produce to God. But, starting with the Last Supper on Holy Thursday, Jesus instituted a new covenant with the Holy Sacrifice of the Mass in a non-bloody sacrifice. The beautiful paintings and stained-glass windows depicting Jesus at a table with bread and wine with his disciples around him commemorates the Last Supper on Holy Thursday.

Our liturgical or Church calendar divides the year into ordinary time and Church seasons such as Advent, Christmas, Lent, and Easter. Liturgy is another word for Eucharistic celebration or Mass. There are different colors that are used in the various seasons, such as, green for ordinary time, violet for Advent, and also white, rose, and black. We have a "lectionary" which is an excerpt of readings from the Bible. Most Masses have three readings: one from the Gospel, one from the Old Testament, and one non-Gospel New Testament. These readings are in three cycles that last three years, and then it repeats.

Many parishes use seasonal missalettes, which I save and hand out to the returnees. When I first started Catholics Returning Home, my presentation on the Mass was walking them through the seasonal missalette and they loved it. So, you certainly can help them understand the Mass by simply going through the seasonal missalette with them. The topics covered in the order of the Mass in the seasonal missalette are:

1) Introductory Rite: Entrance, Greeting, Penitential Act, Gloria, Collect,

2) Liturgy of the Word, First Reading, Responsorial Psalm, Second Reading, Gospel Acclamation, Gospel Reading, Homily, Profession of Faith, Prayers of the Faithful,

3) Liturgy of Eucharist, Presentation and Preparation of the Gifts, Prayer Over Offerings, Eucharistic Prayer, Communion Rite,

4) Concluding Rites, Final Blessing, Dismissal.

The seasonal missalettes have a lot of songs and prayers in addition to the Mass, so they're very useful and helpful to the returnees. Always keep in mind that you're working with "beginner-level, grade-school" people in adult bodies. Thus, if you've ever taught PSR or CCD to grade schoolers, you should be right at home. Even if they went to Catholic school through college, most of the returnees somehow missed the essence of it, or forgot it somewhere along the line. So, you're on very safe ground to assume they're about sixth grade! A walk through the seasonal missalette is just about their right level of understanding.

Other options are:

- A priest can do a "walk through" or explanation of the Mass,
- A staff person or one or more team members can do a "walk through" explanation of the structure and components of the Mass, or a thirty-minute video on the Mass will suffice.

After the presentation or video, discuss any comments or questions. In addition, it's really informative to walk around the inside of the church and explain the various parts of the church. It doesn't have to be overly technical, just explain all the things that you know about, such as the holy water fonts, the tabernacle, the votive light, the statue of Mary, genuflecting outside the pew, the altar, Stations of the Cross, and other statues. You know so much more than the returnees, so you should feel confident, for I've found that the returnees love it. The most important part of the walk-through Mass or explanation of the Mass is to help them feel comfortable and at home in church and with the Mass. The presentation should use basic, grade-school terms.

The closing Our Father should be led around the altar if possible for all who care to join in.

# Session #5
# Explanation of the Sacrament
# of Penance/Confession

- Checklist for Sessions 1-6 from Chapter 5, Session #1

### CHECKLIST FOR SESSION 5 ONLY:

- Schedule one or more team members or other presenters to give an explanation of Penance/Confession, or
- Show a thirty-minute video
- Have DVD and TV set up and ready to go
- Handout for Examination of Conscience (see pages 122-123)
- Motto: When in doubt, err on the side of compassion

Begin with the Prayer of Thomas Merton (see page 99) for all who care to participate. If you have a priest or other presenter available to give an explanation of the Sacrament of Confession, introduce them to the group. Otherwise, you can have one or more team members explain the Sacrament of Penance/Confession and/or watch a thirty-minute video. If you're in or near the church, show them the confessional. Answer any questions related to the Sacrament of Penance.

The approach should be pastoral rather than theoretical or dogmatic. Many people who have been away from the Church are petrified of the Sacrament of Confession. They're afraid they're going to be yelled at. Many have been away for years and don't even know where to begin in trying to remember what they've done or not done.

Some folks have suggested we offer the Sacrament of Confession to the returnees during the session. I have tried having a priest available to them for the sacrament on an optional basis, but it wasn't very well received. Instead, many felt coerced and pressured into going to confession. Accordingly, I don't recommend offering confession during the series but instead letting the returnees follow through on their own. After all, they need to make their own adult decisions, especially with regard to going to confession.

The Sacrament of Confession is also called Penance and the sacrament of conversion, reconciliation, and healing. The Sacrament of the Sick, which is given to people facing surgery or with chronic or grave illnesses, is also a sacrament of healing and reconciliation, and symbolizes Jesus as the Divine physician restoring and healing our hearts and souls. The Sacrament of Reconciliation started with Jesus' own words in John 20:21-23:

> "Peace be with you...As the father has sent me, so I send you. Then he breathed on them and said: 'Receive the Holy spirit. If you forgive men's sins, they are forgiven them; if you hold them bound, they are held bound.'"

After Jesus' resurrection, he spent time with his disciples until his Ascension. With these words in John's

Gospel, he gave them the power to forgive sin. This has been continued to the ordained priests to date with the Sacrament of Holy Orders. The early Church had the "order of penitents" where people once in their lives could repent for grave sins by doing public sacrifice and reparation. Hundreds of years later, the Church started a private form of confession which evolved into the pre-Vatican type of confession, anonymous and behind a screen.

After Vatican II, the focus of confession changed to the sacrament of healing and reconciliation with the focus more on our primary relationship with a loving God and our loving conversion response. More like a loving father/child relationship rather than a distant, stern, authoritarian father. Jesus called his Father "Abba" which is more like "Daddy" and conveys a more intimate, close, warm relationship.

The elements of the celebration of the Sacrament of Penance are: 1) Greeting and blessing from the priest, 2) Priest reading the word of God related to contrition and repentance, 3) Confession of sins, 4) Priest gives the penance, 5) Priest's absolution, 6) Prayer of thanksgiving and praise with dismissal and blessing from priest. This is generally what all parishes do, but they're all somewhat different.

There are two common forms of penance today, one-on-one or communal with the opportunity to go one-on-one. With one-on-one confession, you can either kneel behind a screen or go around and sit face to face with the priest. Many parishes also have "communal penance services" where they have a group gathering service with readings, penitential prayers, songs, and then for those who prefer, they can also go to individual penance for more serious sins. The communal penance services are designed to emphasize the communal nature of sin, because sin hurts not only ourselves but others.

Most parishes have cards or pamphlets near the confessional to aid the penitent with examining their conscience and confessing their sins. Best to get copies of any of those handouts, study them, reflect and pray on them to prepare for reconciliation. They generally cover the two great commandments and the golden rule:

> The Great Commandment.
> "'Which is the first of all the commandments?' Jesus replied: 'This is the first: Hear, O Israel! The Lord our God is Lord alone! Therefore you shall love the Lord your God with all your heart, with all your soul, with all your mind, and with all your strength. This is the second: You shall love your neighbor as yourself. There is no other commandment greater than these'" (Mark 12:28-31).

> Golden Rule.
> "Treat others the way you would have them treat you: this sums up the law and the prophets" (Matthew 7:12).

Most parishes offer reconciliation at certain times, you can check your parish bulletin or website. Or, you can make an appointment with a priest. Read and reflect on the parish handout for examination of conscience and reconciliation. Especially reflect on the two great commandments and the Golden Rule. When you get your nerve up, go into the reconciliation room, either behind the screen or around the curtain face to face. First thing is to tell the priest you've been away a long time and ask him for help. Like the Good Shepherd, I've always found priests to be very happy and jubilant about helping someone return after being gone a long time.

In order for someone to decide to return to church after a long absence, it takes the Lord's grace touching their heart, and a huge act of conversion to make that change. Some fear ridicule from others. Others struggle with their feelings of unworthiness and guilt. Some feel they've committed "unforgiveable" sins and they're excommunicated and they can't return. Those are all temptations because the Lord wants all to return. For many, even after returning to attend church, they are still very fearful of going to confession.

In order to commit a serious sin it must be a serious matter, you must know it's a serious matter, and you must freely choose to do it. But, no matter what, all sins can be forgiven with conversion, repentance, and contrition. One can always turn to the Lord and be saved. The Lord wants and wills that all come to repentance and be saved. Remember Saint Dismas, the good thief, who was one of the two men that was crucified with Jesus. After he repented and turned to the Lord, Jesus told him that "today you'll be with me in Paradise!" (Luke 23:43). Surely we can take the Lord's own words to heart!

Close this session with a prayer and gather everyone around the altar (if possible) and pray the Our Father.

# Session #6
# Wrap-up, Evaluation, and Discussion of the Creed

- Checklist for Sessions 1-6 from Chapter 5, Session #1

### CHECKLIST FOR SESSION 6 ONLY:

- Optional video on the Creed
- Have DVD and TV set up and ready to go
- Copies of the Nicene Creed with explanation of the Creed
- Blank evaluation forms

The purpose of the final session is to close out the series, affirm the attendees for participating, and assure them they are on a lifelong journey which is only just beginning. In addition, the attendees are asked to complete an evaluation form and invited to become involved with the Catholics Returning Home ministry and/or guided into other adult faith offerings. Lastly, the Nicene Creed is discussed and explained in an effort to help the returnees become more comfortable with their faith.

The leader welcomes all attendees and says he/she's going to read the Prayer of Thomas Merton (see page 99), for all who care to participate.

### JUST THE BEGINNING

The leader informs the returnees that although this is the last session, it's still only the beginning of their journey with the Church. They're welcome to come back for the next series and bring others along. At this point, ask the returnees to complete the evaluation form (see page 124) which has the following questions: 1) What did you like about the series? 2) Suggestions for improving the series? 3) Would you be willing to participate in the ministry as follows: a) Participating on the planning team? b) Attending ongoing sessions and sharing your story? or other comments.

Explain that the input from these forms will help future Catholics Returning Home teams with their feedback. Tell them their help is needed to help other returnees. Ask them to remember how comfortable and at ease they felt when they heard other team members share their experiences of being away and returning to the Church. In the same way, they can help themselves and others by being willing to share their own stories. Really encourage them to consider being involved and on the team. Give them about ten minutes to complete the evaluation and then collect them.

Distribute any additional parish information such as bulletins, booklets, and so on that describes parish activities and scheduled services. Encourage them to check out the other ministries in the parish, especially Bible study and other small-group activities such as my book *Catholics Continuing the Journey: A Faith-Sharing Program for Small Groups*. Tell them the team members will be happy to help them look into any of these other ministries if they need help.

### THE NICENE CREED AND EXPLANATION

If you choose to use an optional video on the Creed, play the video and discuss it. You can also give them a copy of the Nicene Creed that includes an explanation.

If you don't use a video, tell the returnees that in continuing their journey in the Church it's time to think a bit more about what they believe. The Nicene Creed is the foundation of what Catholics believe and this is the night the group is going to discuss the Creed. Ask the group to look at the sheet that shows the Creed and its explanation. Next, go around the room in order and have each person read a phrase and its explanation. Then, that person can make a comment, ask a question, relate it to their own lives, or attempt to define it in their own words. It's fine to say that much of the Creed is mystery and accepted by faith. In my experience, some of the most profound and touching beliefs have been expressed by returnees in this format.

At one group, we had a pair of women who seemed to hang on to their insecurities throughout the series. When we got to the last evening and the discussion of the Creed, I handed out the Creed with explanation sheet and told them we would be discussing and reflecting on it in order to help them understand it in greater depth. At this point, one of the women said that she couldn't discuss the Creed since it had too many big words and she lacked the proper religious education. She was indignant that I was even asking her to do such a thing. However, she said that even though she wasn't qualified to discuss the Creed, she would take the last line which said, "Amen, so be it," because she believed it with all her heart! All of us in the room were taken aback by her great expression of faith. She didn't have to say any more than that, because what else could be said? She had said it all!

### SAYING GOOD-BYE

End the session on time! Thank the returnees again for attending, invite them back for the next series, and encourage them to bring others with them. If anyone wants to join in the closing prayer, they're welcome to do so.

After praying the Our Father, the team should stay for a while, answering questions and talking with returnees. Some of the returnees will not want to leave, especially after the last session. This is a great accomplishment. It's better to have them want more than to drop out because they feel the series has run too long.

### FOLLOW-UP SESSIONS AND ONGOING SUPPORT

The most important aspect of Catholics Returning Home is the small-group faith sharing and storytelling. Those returning are able to relate, bond, and be accepted by program team members in a small-group faith community. By sharing their faith journeys, the returnees are able to let go of their fears and failures and develop trust within the parish community. Only then are they ready, willing, and open enough to seek and accept updated information about Catholic Christianity.

The catechetical content is designed to be an update of the basics of Catholicism for adults taught at a grade-school level. Many returnees left as teenagers or young adults and never acquired an adult understanding or appreciation of their faith. The six-week series is designed to welcome them back, help them overcome their difficulties with the Church, facilitate development of trust in the faith community, and then update them on the basics of Catholicism in order to help them reattach and bond.

Much is accomplished in that six weeks in order to move people from being totally separated from the Church to feeling comfortable and at home with a working knowledge of the basics. Most of the returnees say they want the series to continue beyond the six weeks. After the six-week series, you can meet as "graduates of CRH" as needed on other faith update topics of interest. Sometimes I meet with them to study the *YouCat*, which is the youth Catechism. Other groups wanted to study the lectionary readings for the week. And, others picked topics of interest such as Mary and the saints, prayer, and so forth. In addition, you can follow up with *Catholics Continuing the Journey: A Faith-Sharing Program for Small Groups* that I wrote. It's a six-week spiritual development and formation series that focuses on their relationship with God and others.

However, Catholics Returning Home itself must stay as originally designed so it can continue to attract and help the returnees that are a long way off and totally detached and adrift. A miracle occurs in the attendees in the space of six weeks. They grow and develop in their faith life to the point that they are hungry for more. It's critical that graduated returnees be channeled into special update sessions for "graduates of CRH" or other ministries in the parish where they can continue their journey of faith development. They should be included on the mailing lists for upcoming adult faith offerings as well. It's critical that we carefully guide and foster their reattachment while still letting them make their own adult choices. After all, the goal is for them to be adult, mature disciples joining us on the mission.

Recommended ministries for ongoing support and enrichment include those for the divorced/remarried, annulment process, bereavement, Bible study, and other small-group faith communities. Be sure to make available an index of the various parish ministries that lists the names of the contact persons. Returnees feel wanted and part of the parish family if they become personally involved with the Church in some way. In addition, some Catholics Returning Home teams periodically call past attendees and maintain contact with them, answering any questions they may have and providing a much needed "life line" to the Church.

The attendees' comments from the evaluation forms are overwhelmingly positive and they are grateful for the series. They appreciate the personal attention, time spent, warmth, and sharing. Many say they want to have more sessions and information. Again, that is a miracle to behold to see the change that the Lord works within them in six short weeks. And, we do need to cater to their needs for ongoing formation whether in additional sessions for the "graduates of CRH" or to channel them to other adult faith offerings. But, the original six-week series of Catholics Returning Home must stay as it is to continue focusing on and serving those who are the farthest away so as to attract and help the most needy.

# Handout for Session #3

## Pre-Vatican II and Post-Vatican II
### Differences after Vatican II
### Refocusing on Individual from Institutional

I.    Bible Study Groups

II.   Diaconate (Back to Roots)
   A. Baptism
   B. Weddings
   C. Funerals
   D. Service to Community

III.  Lay Ministry

IV.   Lay Involvement in the Liturgy
   A. Eucharistic Ministers
   B. Contemporary Mass
   C. Liturgy Commission
   D. Laity involvement in writing of the liturgies
   E. Laity – Decorating the Altar

V.    Confession to Reconciliation

VI.   Mass
   A. Local Language
   B. Removal of Communion Rail
   C. Priest Faces Congregation
   D. Congregational Participation

# Handout for Session #5
# Examination of Conscience

## AM I AT PEACE WITH MYSELF?

- Am I honest with myself at all times?
- Am I patient with myself?
- Do I brood over my failings?
- Have I forgiven myself for my sins and shortcomings?
- Am I still growing, developing?
- Am I set in my ways, unwilling to change?
- Do I take care of myself? Physically? Spiritually?

## AM I AT PEACE WITH OTHERS?

What disrupts the harmony that should exist between myself and ...

- My spouse?
- My children?
- My parents?
- My relatives?
- My friends?
- My neighbors?

## DO I DEAL JUSTLY WITH OTHERS, GIVING THEM WHAT IS DUE THEM?

- My employers?
- My employees?
- My fellow workers?

## AM I AT PEACE WITH GOD?

- What disrupts the harmony He wants to exist between us?
- Do I see God as a lawgiver and judge or as a loving, merciful Savior?
- Have I allowed other things or persons to take His place in my life?
- Have I thanked Him for His endless compassion and limitless love?

## AM I AT PEACE WITH THE WORLD?

- Do I see the world as something given to me and all persons that will come after me as a trust?
- Have I abused its resources?
- Am I wasteful: With money? With the things I use? With my time? With others' time?
- Must I always have the latest? The best?
- Do I feel responsibility for my community? Do I vote? Have I volunteered to help?

## EVALUATION FORM WEEK #6                DATE: _____

1. What did you like about the series?

a)

_____

_____

b)

_____

_____

c)

_____

_____

2. Suggestions for improving the sessions?

a)

_____

_____

b)

_____

_____

c)

_____

_____

3. Would you be willing to participate in the ministry as follows?

|  | YES | NO |
|---|---|---|
| a) Participating on the planning team? | ☐ | ☐ |
| b) Attending on-going sessions and sharing your story? | ☐ | ☐ |

c) Other comments:

_____

_____

_____

Name, Phone #

# Handout for Session #6

| Nicene Creed | Explanation |
|---|---|
| I believe in one God | Three Persons – One God |
| The Father Almighty, Maker of heaven and earth, of all things visible and invisible. | 1ˢᵗ Person of the Trinity; Creator of ALL that which is known or unknown. |
| I believe in One Lord, Jesus Christ, the only Begotten SON of God, born of the Father before all ages, God from God, Light from light, True God from True God, begotten not made, consubstantial with the Father. Through Him all things were made. | 2ⁿᵈ Person of the Trinity; Son, Redeemer; this tells us His relationship to the 1st Person; He is equal to the Father. |
| For us men and for OUR salvation He came down from heaven and by the Holy Spirit was incarnate of the Virgin Mary and became Man. | The 2ⁿᵈ Person of the Trinity took on humanity in the person of Jesus. |
| For OUR sake He was crucified under Pontius Pilate; He suffered death, and was buried and rose again on the third day in accordance with the scriptures. He ascended into heaven and is seated at the right hand of the Father. | Summarizes the Paschal (Easter) Mystery. We recall this at Mass during the Memorial Acclamation. He rose from the dead, body, and soul; He returned to the Father as Jesus, 2ⁿᵈ Person of the Trinity, human and divine. |

| | |
|---|---|
| He will come AGAIN in glory to JUDGE the living and the dead, and His kingdom will have no end. | The Second Coming of Christ. The Final judgement at the end of time. |
| I believe in the Holy Spirit, the Lord, the Giver of life, who proceeds from the Father and the Son, who with the Father and the Son He is adored and glorified, who has spoken through the prophets. | 3rd Person of the Trinity; Sanctifier; Relationship to the 1st and 2nd Persons of the Trinity; Equal with the Father and the Son; Source of inspiration for the scriptures. |
| I believe in one, holy, catholic, and apostolic Church. | United in Creed, Code and Worship. Holy because Jesus is holy. Universal, founded on the Apostles. |
| I confess one Baptism for the forgiveness of sins. | Initiation into the Body of Christ. |
| And I look forward to the Resurrection of the dead, and the Life of the world to come. | We will also rise from the dead, body and soul like Jesus. Eternal life – Heaven or Hell. |
| Amen. | "So be it!" Statement of affirmation and acceptance. |

## Chapter 7

# A Final Word of Encouragement

I started this ministry many years ago after I decided that "somebody" needed to do something about all the people who had drifted away from their Catholic faith, and the Lord convinced me that I was that "somebody." It's been utterly amazing to see how this ministry has spread everywhere and helped so many people return to their Catholic faith. It's been an honor and a privilege to be part of this wonderful work of grace from the Lord. I treasure all the friends I've met everywhere who have shared their life stories with me, and I'm humbled and awed that I have been allowed to witness and share in their faith journeys. It's been a joy and privilege! But, our work is far from done. The harvest is ready and we need more workers in the vineyards! But, thankfully Catholics Returning Home has become a classic, time-tested, proven ministerial tool to help even more people return. Praise Jesus, the Good Shepherd, for showing us the way!

## Chapter 8

# Program Resources

### VIDEOS

*Stories of Faith from Catholics Returning Home.*
Thirty-minute video for week 2. Order from Deacon
John Rex, Lighthouse Printing, call 708-479-7776 or
send an email to jrex@lighthouseprinting.net, https://
lighthouseprinting.net/catholics-returning-home/

*Vatican II in History.* Hallel Videos. https://hallelvideos.
com/

Liguori Publications has videos on the Mass and Reconciliation, www.liguori.org

RCL Benziger has videos on the Creed,
*I Believe/We Believe*, https://www.rclbenziger.com/

## BOOKS

*Catechism of the Catholic Church.*

*Catholics Continuing the Journey: A Faith-Sharing Program for Small Groups,* by Sally Mews.

*Handbook for Catholics,* Mary Kathleen Glavich, SND.

*Returning Home to Your Catholic Faith,* by Sally Mews.

*Sent Forth in the Spirit: A Confirmation Text for Adults,* by Patricia Mann, Ph.D. Resource for adult Confirmation preparation.

*YouCat,* Youth Catechism.

## SIGNS AND BANNERS

To order from Deacon John Rex, Lighthouse Printing, call 708-479-7776, or send an email to jrex@ lighthouseprinting.net, https://lighthouseprinting.net/ catholics-returning-home/

## WEBSITES

http://www.catholicsreturninghome.org

https://lighthouseprinting.net/catholics-returning-home/

For seminars and speaking engagements, contact Sally Mews at 715-254-0935, or email: ssmews@msn.com

### Letter of Understanding and Agreement

Your use of "Catholics Returning Home (CRH)" program, name, and logo by Sally L. Mews acknowledges your agreement to abide by the following requirements:

1. CRH is copyrighted; thus, Sally L. Mews owns all rights in the program and content. Additionally, since CRH was recognized by the USCCB in "A Time to Listen…A Time to Heal" as a model program for reaching out to non-practicing Catholics, Sally L. Mews wants to maintain the integrity of the CRH name and program.

2. CRH is time tested and proven; thus, it is to be used in its entirety as designed. Please do not change the content, design, or name of the CRH program.

3. If you make substantial changes to CRH and create your own program, then please do not use the CRH name or logo. In this instance, if you "draw" from the CRH program, your creation must be substantially different in content, design, and name so as not to be confused with CRH. In addition, you should acknowledge your source as being from CRH.

4. Please let Sally L. Mews know if you have any questions or comments concerning the use of CRH.

5. The only requirement for the use of CRH, including all the materials, handouts, and logo, is to follow it as designed. Contact Sally L. Mews for a copy of the black and white logo that can be reproduced.

Sally L. Mews
Founder/Director of Catholics Returning Home
ssmews@msn.com
PH: 715-254-0935
http://www.catholicsreturninghome.org

## Testimonials

I was a recently returned Catholic, who had been away from the Church for 25 years, when I saw the ad for Catholics Returning Home. I was hungry for more knowledge and education about my faith and signed up PRONTO. I'm so grateful I did. The program is concise and gets directly to the matters at hand. We are able to get our questions answered, our fears and inhibitions about returning addressed, and updated on what changes have occurred since we've been away. It's like a 101-prep course for what's up ahead—a life with the Lord and a new family! I'm so glad I went through the program and would recommend it to anyone considering the next step. I'm also grateful to have Sally and husband Skip in my own home town!

*Lorelei Walczak*
*Stevens Point, Wisconsin*

THE ROMAN CATHOLIC CHURCH
# DIOCESE OF TUCSON
64 EAST BROADWAY BOULEVARD
P.O. Box 31 • Tucson, Arizona 85702-0031
520-838-2500 • Fax: 520-838-2590 • www.diocesetucson.org

OFFICE OF THE BISHOP

May 1, 2017

TO WHOM IT MAY CONCERN:

It is a pleasure to write a letter of recommendation for Mrs. Sally Mews, who has done great work with her "Welcome Home" program. This outreach to alienated Catholics was begun by Sally many years ago, when seemingly, no one was talking about it. However, since she herself was once an alienated Catholic, she knew the pain and the longing to rejoin the body of Christ.

Singlehandedly, with the supervision of her pastor at St. Joseph's Parish in Libertyville, she began those little steps that have now become a trailblazing program which she has conducted in many parishes and dioceses around the country including in our Diocese of Tucson.

The program grew and grew, so that many people have returned to the Church. There is a long list of parishes which have asked Sally to assist them to welcome home our brothers and sisters.

Her program is faithful to Catholic teaching and I am confident she will assist you in welcoming alienated Catholics back to the Church.

Sincerely yours in Christ,

*+ Gerald Kicanas*

Most Rev. Gerald F. Kicanas, D.D.
Bishop of Tucson

I am so appreciative of the Catholics Returning Home program. It is a true gift to all who participate, offering them an opportunity to learn more about the faith, have their questions answered, their concerns alleviated, and to experience a welcome home like no other. It's presented in a loving, judgement-free, no-pressure environment and I am proud to be a volunteer for the program in my local parish.

*Sondra Hebert*
*Lafayette, Louisiana*

My wife and I have been using the Catholics Returning Home program for three years, taking over the leadership from another couple who had lead it for ten years.

We have found the sessions are just the right presentation to encourage those seeking to return to an active faith life. The program is an informative, non-threatening path back to the Church. We highly recommend this program for our lost brothers and sisters seeking a way home.

*Deacon Ray Arnold*
*Our Lady of Mercy, Redding, California*

---

### ARCHDIOCESE OF CHICAGO

Most Reverend Gerald F. Kicanas
Auxiliary Bishop of Chicago
Episcopal Vicar of Vicariate I
Phone: 847/549-0160

200 North Milwaukee Avenue
Suite 200
Libertyville, Illinois 60048
FAX: 847/549-0163

January, 2000

TO WHOM IT MAY CONCERN

It is a pleasure to write a letter of recommendation for **Mrs. Sally Mews**, who has done great work with her "Welcome Home" program. This outreach to alienated Catholics was begun by Sally many years ago, when seemingly, no one was talking about it. However, since she herself was once an alienated Catholic, she knew the pain and the longing to rejoin the body of Christ.

Singlehandedly, with the supervision of her pastor at St. Joseph's Parish in Libertyville, she began those little steps that have now become a trailblazing program. At her own expense, she would print up flyers and contact media people to widen her reach. The program grew and grew, so that today, just in my own Vicariate, which includes all of Lake County, there is a long list of parishes which have asked Sally to assist them to welcome home our brothers and sisters.

Always working under the guidance of the parish pastoral staff, this assured all concerned that the information handed on was the authentic teaching of the Church. One of the primary reasons for the grand success of Sally's program is that she has had many years to fine tune it, and as a result, we offer a program that has stood the test of time.

If you require further information, please call me.

Sincerely yours in Christ,

+ Gerald Kicanas

Most Reverend Gerald F. Kicanas
Auxiliary Bishop of Chicago

:mh!

Since 2002 the Catholics Returning Home program has given parishes in Australia the courage and confidence to reach out to inactive Catholics. It continues to meet a pressing need in the Australian Church today.

I know of no comparable program that is as practical, healing and compassionate as CRH. Sally has accomplished something great for God, ensuring that each person who comes to a CRH session is welcomed and surrounded by love.

CRH is clear and simple and born out of Sally's practical experience. Its simplicity and the normality of the approach makes it especially helpful.

*Jan Heath, "Evangelise Now"*
*Our Lady of the Way Parish*
*Queensland, Australia*

As a cradle Catholic growing up in a small Midwestern town, my parents took my siblings and I to Mass each Sunday, ensured we had a Catholic education through the parish CCD program, and received the Sacraments of Initiation at the proper ages. My mother belonged to the Altar and Rosary society and my father was a Knight. We grew up with a priest coming over for dinner once or twice a month. But even with this good exposure to Catholic formation, my siblings and I all stopped practicing our Catholic faith.

Upon graduating from college, I moved to St. Louis and married my husband. I had a great job and loved city life. I was living the American dream but there was something missing from my life. I was too busy living to really consider what. It was not until my first child was born and I wanted to have her baptized that I began to reflect on my relationship with God. I had been gone for fifteen years but began to go to Mass. I would skip Easter and Christmas Mass because it irritated me that I could not find a seat. My relationship with God was really "Sunday only." I did not allow this Sunday experience to impact my personal life.

My family continued to grow but my returning to the Church was causing strife in my marriage. At the same time that my marriage was unraveling, my relationship with God was growing. Our family moved to a very small town in Illinois where I registered my children in CCD. Not long after, I became a single parent trying to raise four kids in the faith. My pastor asked me to lead a Catholics Returning Home program in our parish and my response was, "Father, how can I? I don't know my faith." His response was, "I'll help you." Our parish used Catholics Returning Home, advertising in the local papers, and had a billboard made for a busy highway between our small town and the city where many in our community worked. Our small rural parish had 20 people return to the faith that fall. This experience led me to teaching Confirmation, then RCIA, and eventual employment in the Church. I took on greater and greater responsibility in the Church as my relationship with God moved beyond a "Sunday only" thing to daily prayer, volunteering in Church and community ministries, and sharing why I was Catholic with people I met.

I have learned a lot about my faith by leading and teaching others. I learned not only about God but about a relationship with God and His Church and how it should be lived. I am still working for the Church. I am the Director of Evangelization and Catechesis for a large Catholic Church in Texas. God taught me to let go and rely on Him. I am blessed and very thankful to God for returning home.

*Dawn Ward*
*Arlington, Texas*


The unique feature of the Catholics Returning Home program is that it is the fruit of the life experience of Sally Mews. She had drifted from parish sacramental life. She discovered how difficult it was to return to a Sunday parish community where no one even noticed she had been gone. So this program evolved from one who struggled to return and who became motivated to produce a simple, sympathetic and practical short program that enables people to express their hurts and their struggles on their spiritual journey. It springs from a lay person and is best run by lay people for lay people; it is for those adults who are drawn into taking another look at becoming a disciple of Jesus in our ever old but ever renewing Catholic Church.

*Fr. Paul G. Shannahan sm, former National Director*
*of the Catholic Enquiry Centre, Wellington, and now*
*parish priest of Akaroa, New Zealand*


Sally Mews provides a vital direction in ministry to our brothers and sisters in Christ, who have found themselves wandering in a wilderness that has caused them to be disconnected in some manner from sharing in the full richness of God's One, Holy, Catholic, and Apostolic Church. The format of Catholics Returning Home provides a tangible means for those who have been "disconnected" from the Church for whatever reason, to reconnect and re-establish a meaningful and fulfilling relationship, first with Jesus Christ, our Redeemer, God our Father, and the Holy Spirit, followed by recognizing that all humanity is on the same journey, where the paths we follow, hopefully lead us to share common bonds in faith, hope, and love for the sake of having abundant life together in Christ.

*Deacon Art Schaller*
*St. Stephen & St. Joseph Parishes*
*Diocese of La Crosse, Stevens Point, Wisconsin*

I have been involved with Catholics Returning Home since we started the program several years ago at St Pius X in Lafayette, Louisiana. Initially, my main reason for helping was to support my daughter who had been away from the Church in college, and I was afraid she would back out if someone wasn't there for her. After the first six-week session, I was enamored by the whole process and felt it was a very worthy ministry to be involved in.

As I participated in more sessions, I found myself getting excited as I watched the growth that happens over the weeks and how the Holy Spirit works in and through us and touches those who are attending. Sometimes, they not only return to church but also become on fire for their faith. And that is an awesome experience to behold.

Since every group of participants is very different, all of our sessions are quite varied, even though the format/outline remains the same, because we have very different discussions that come out. And many of us, facilitators and participants alike, learn something new every time. It is very invigorating and we all grow in some way or another. As the years have passed, the Holy Spirit has taken my innately shy nature and participation as a "supportive bystander" to being the leader of the sessions and becoming more and more outspoken. And I have peace within me—that the Holy Spirit will provide the message that needs to be heard each particular evening—at least that is my prayer. Being involved in this program is very special to me and I am humbled by the way it all works out.

*Phyllis Comeaux*
*Lafayette, Louisiana*

My parents were Catholic (my mother converted as an adult) and I attended both public and Catholic grade schools and, when in high school, was a freshman at a Jesuit boys school. I then transferred to a public school for the last three years. And it was not long after I changed high schools that I stopped attending Mass or otherwise practicing my religion.

I am 76 years old now and did not feel the need to explore a return to the faith until about eight years ago. In the meantime, I was married and had two sons. Over the years, I was successful in a number of challenging jobs. At home, my wife and I faced a difficult situation because our older son was brain damaged as a baby and needed to be carefully watched and cared for 24 hours a day. We spent many years searching out therapies that might help him and letting him experience as normal a life as possible.

My wife and I divorced in 2000. I continued to be a big part of both my sons' lives and to be available to help with my older son's care. Our older boy, after struggling with liver problems, died in 2013 at the age of 47. I remain close to my younger son and his family—his lovely wife and delightful granddaughter.

It was an unusual event that triggered my return to the Church, or least it seems so to me. I was listening, as I frequently do, to talk radio, and heard a program that described the significance of the washing of Jesus' feet. The speaker explained the practical and spiritual significance of the act in a way I had not appreciated before. At the end of the program, the speaker provided a way to contact an ecumenical organization for ex-Catholics who were interested in returning to the Church.

I called the number and discovered that the person I should talk to, Sally Mews, happened to be temporarily in the Phoenix area, where I live. It was a long drive to meet up with Sally and her husband (about 50 miles), but I am grateful that I made the trip. Sally explained how the Church had changed over the years, both as to how Mass was conducted and in its openness to change, such as providing women a greater role in worship and decision making.

After we talked, we all attended Mass and I was able to experience the changes myself. English language. Music. Meaningful and helpful sermon.

I then began the process of examining my relationship to Jesus and to the Catholic faith. I have not missed Sunday Mass for almost eight years. I regularly go to confession. In fact, the process of confession has helped me resolve, after several years, a longstanding pain and sense of betrayal I had harbored for many years.

I think God made Sally available to me at the point in time that I needed her and was ready to open myself to her guidance. I was in the right place at the right time, and was able to let her start my recovery of faith.

I end on a note of thanks—to Sally Mews for her outreach to people like me. And to God for providing the path for my return.

*Michael Leahy*
*Scottsdale, Arizona*

I grew up in a small middle-class home at the south end of Jefferson Street in Abbeville, Louisiana. It was a time just before color TVs, when you could still go to sleep at night with the doors open to let the breeze flow through the house. My mother was raised in the Catholic faith, my father was not. I lived one block from the elementary school. Behind that school was a very non-descript building where all the kids dutifully reported once each week according to grade level. It was the building where we received catechism. We spent mornings before school with the nuns learning how to be good Catholic children and prepared ourselves to receive the sacraments for the first time. To this day, I can still remember walking across the grass of the broad expanse of playground to the little building.

As a teenage I attended Mass mostly by myself, riding my bike on Sundays through the neighborhoods to the center of town where St. Mary Magdalene Catholic church still stands today. It was, and is a magnificent church building, a center piece for the quite little town in which I grew up. As I grew, for reasons I can't even remember, I stopped going. I had friends who attended regularly, but I lost my way. Through the years, I've had this urge to find my way back, but couldn't find the path. As an adult, I've driven past St. Pius X several thousand times and have admired the little round church under the beautiful oaks.

Now, I'm married to a wonderful woman who's my best friend. One of our mutual goals in our marriage was to find what Debbie calls "a home church." A place to receive the word of God, a place to receive comfort, a place to serve, place of welcome. Debbie was raised in the Baptist faith, and me, well I was a non-practicing Catholic at that point in time. So off we went, in search of our church home. One religion was just way too loud for me; the rock-and-roll band just wasn't my idea of church. Another was just too mild, somewhat Catholic, but just not right. Then, I spotted the Catholics Returning Home banner hanging under the beautiful oaks of St. Pius X Church. I jotted down the number and Debbie called and met Ashton Mouton. Turns out we have friends in common with Ashton; a good sign. We made arrangements to attend the first meeting of the Catholics Returning Home session, and after a bit of hunting to find the right room we are greeted with a warm "welcome."

Debbie and I began attending Mass right away. For me, sitting in the pew and being part of the Mass was truly a return home. After attending a service that was too loud, and one that was not quite right, this experience at St. Pius was just right. Kind of like putting on an old, comfortable pair of shoes. Not that the Catholic religion is an old pair of shoes, but I think we can all relate to the meaning; this was just right, a comfortable fit. Debbie even attended RCIA and last Easter Vigil received the Sacrament of Communion for the first time as a member of the Catholic faith. Throughout the process of both Catholics Returning Home and RCIA, we both experienced the wonderful feeling of "welcome."

How wonderful it is to be part of this Year of Mercy and slip on the comfortable pair of shoes and cross the threshold into the grace of Jesus Christ as members of the Catholic religion and parishioners of St. Pius X Catholic church. Welcome.

*Pat Attaway*
*Lafayette, Louisiana*


...Catholic Relief Services (CRS), [is] a U.S. Catholic organization that works in 101 countries around the world to provide relief during emergencies and to promote development, justice and peace. [The] President and CEO of CRS, has asked us to reach out to Catholics Returning Home and other organizations to learn about effective ways to promote awareness and build engagement among our audiences in the United States. Catholics Returning Home is seen as a leader in this area!

It would be very helpful if you would be willing to share your insights about how Catholics Returning Home builds awareness and engages audiences during a 30-minute phone interview.

*Catholic Relief Services, July 2016*

I completed the CRH program at my parish. It went very well! We had 2 participants. We used your program the way it is designed. The videos were great and everyone got a lot out of them. Participation in the discussion after the videos was constructive.

It's so easy to do. I was amazed! I'm looking for some open dates after Easter to do it again.

Thank you so much for all you do.

*Shelly Orr*
*Queen of Angels Parish, Port Angeles, Washington*

Many Catholic parishes find the outreach ministry to Catholics who have become, for whatever reason, estranged from the Church to be challenging to the point of neglect. They may feel they have neither the people resources, nor the tools, in place to successfully carry on this ministry in a truly welcoming and non-judgmental way. The RCIA program was not necessarily meant to address feelings of guilt and hurt of so called "fallen away Catholics" who had previously been catechized and received sacraments of initiation.

Sally Mews has developed a loving and non-intimidating program in Catholics Returning Home (CRH) that addresses the special needs of members of former parish members, living on the fringe, who have a desire to return but have not heard a welcoming invitation or who have not been presented a pathway to come home.

I can attest to the success of her program firsthand, in both its design and how she and her husband partner to carry it out. I attended all six sessions as an observer/aide during a recent year when she graciously offered it in our parish. I certainly hope and pray that many others will adopt her format of healing the wounds and filling gaps in the catechesis of those who are yearning, but perhaps needing the courage, to answer a loving invitation to re-join God's family, the Church.

*Rick Giese*
*Pastoral council president, leader of prayer, retired DRE*
*St. Stephen Parish, Stevens Point, Wisconsin*


I have run Catholics Returning Home at my parish for many years and seen the fruits it produces. There are many programs, books, CDs, and DVDs designed to help bring fallen away Catholics back into a relationship with Christ and His bride the Church. All have good points but I've never experienced a program like CRH. With a team of people, who have a heart for their brothers and sisters who have forgotten where their true home is, with fervent prayer, and if the program is followed as de-signed, souls will be awakened to fall in love again with Jesus. CRH reminds me of 2 Kings, chapter 5, the cure of Naaman. Elisha tells him to go and wash seven times in the Jordan but Naaman goes away angry, thinking the cure proposed to be ridiculously simple. Fortunately for his sake his servant convinced him otherwise. Some may think CRH to be too simple but that is the beauty of this program. Don't underestimate its simplicity; follow the program as designed and let the Holy Spirit take over. They will come home.

*Deacon John Rex*
*Clergy Representative for CRH and serving at*
*St. Damian Parish, Oak Forest, Illinois*

My introduction to CRH occurred at a difficult time in my life. During that time, I reflected on my life and tried to determine when life was more stable and fulfilling. It was at this time that I realized the one thing that was not part of my life was my Faith and Christ. It had been 35 years since I had left the Church.

I decided to make an effort to return to the Church. I had no idea where to begin my journey. I went to churches and picked up brochures and religious booklets with the hope that this would lead me to my Faith. I also attended a Mass and realized that the Church had changed because of Vatican II. Everything was foreign to me and confusing.

One day I saw an advertisement for a program at St. Joseph's church in Libertyville Illinois, entitled "Catholics Returning Home" presented by Sally Mews. I signed up and changed my life forever. The program introduced me to the new Church as defined by Vatican II and took me through the process of regaining my Faith. Sally's presentation was simple and enlightening, my questions were answered and many mysteries solved.

When the program ended, we were invited to attend confession for the absolution of our sins. It was difficult for me to go to confession since it was 35 years since I had left the Church. It was also difficult because of the Vatican II changes, I would be sitting in front of the priest. However, with the help from Sally and Father Ron, my confession was simple and uplifting.

During my confession, Father Ron asked me to confess one sin that I needed to acknowledge. Without any hesitation, I said "I denied Christ." I have no idea where that statement came from and can only believe that the Holy Spirit was with me for guidance.

Since my completion of the CRH program, my journey to Christ continues. In addition to attending Mass, I have been studying the Bible for the past six years. I have also attended yearly sessions with a parish group to study and discuss the Scriptures, using workbooks developed by Catholic biblical scholars. I am also discussing the program with friends who have left the Church with the hope of guiding them back to Christ.

With my new life in the Catholic Church, it is with deep emotion that I express my thanks and gratitude to Sally Mews and the Catholics Returning Home program.

*Richard Krummick*
*St. Raphael's Parish, Oshkosh, Wisconsin*

About eight years ago I was driving along the road and noticed a sign, "Catholics Returning Home Begins Soon," with a phone number to call for more information. That phone call was my savior. I had not gone to Mass in many years. For six weeks, I attended helpful meetings with wonderful people from the parish. One of those meetings explained the Sacrament of Reconciliation which I thought was great. It helped me realize it's not something to be afraid of. I now go to Mass every week and bring Communion to a home-bound person. I'm very thankful to Catholics Returning Home.

*Fran H., a returnee*
*St. Damian Parish, Oak Forest, Illinois*

*The following article is from the United States Conference of Catholic Bishops (USCCB) directory "A Time to Listen...A Time to Heal," May 1999. Catholics Returning Home was listed as a model program. The CRH program is time tested and proven and used throughout the US and other countries.*

CATHOLICS RETURNING HOME

A Ministry of Compassion and Reconciliation—Chicago, Ill.

Catholics Returning Home is an RCIA-like process for reaching out and inviting inactive Catholics to return "home" to the Church and resume an active practice of their faith. It is conducted in a nonjudgmental support-group format. However, a sequence of topics on the basics of Catholicism are covered during the six-week series so that attendees are updated. The process is both formational and informational.

This ministry is a "lay-driven" process that works best in a team environment. A team coordinating the ministry should be composed of both staff and volunteers, including some who have been away from the Church and have returned. Team members need not be "mini-theologians"; however, they should be compassionate and nonjudgmental to returnees. A variety of professional staff and clergy should present the topics.

Minimal resources are necessary because the publicity can be done via free news releases, cable TV, fliers, bulletin articles, and signs. The name "Catholics Returning Home" is very effective in reaching people who have been away from the Church because they identify with the name. People who have been away for years say they came to the sessions because they saw the signs that say "Catholics Returning Home."

There are three major outreaches during the year, each six weeks long: Come Home for Christmas, Come Home for Easter, and Come Home in September. The series' topics are: (1) welcome by the team leader, an open-ended questionnaire, and sharing by team and attendees on "why they are here"; (2) viewing of the Fr. McKee video on returning Catholics and a discussion; (3) explanation of the Church today, including changes since Vatican II; (4) a walk through the Mass and a discussion; (5) "tips on sinning" with an explanation of reconciliation, and confession; and (6) discussion of the Creed, what Catholics believe. All sessions conclude with the Lord's Prayer.

By the end of the series, most of the participants should be comfortable with the Church and seek to be reconnected. Some may want to become involved with ministry to inactive Catholics. Many want to continue with more in-depth adult education/formation sessions such as Bible study. Two or three continuing sessions can be offered in February/March and October/November to cover additional topics and to allow returnees to meet with other Church leaders and parishioners.

The CRH program has been an invitation from heaven, giving me an opportunity to reclaim my Catholic Faith — my deepest gratitude to those who have welcomed me home.

*Comment from a returning Catholic*
*Brisbane, Australia*

When I first read Sally Mews' book, I knew that this was the book that I had been looking for. I had longed to bring friends and family back to our Catholic faith, but had no idea how to go about it systematically. With Sally's nuts and bolts approach, I was able to present the Catholics Returning Home program to my pastor, that was almost seven years ago, and I have loved every minute of bringing Catholics home. I have designated myself "the Good Shepherd's Border Collie." Thank you so much, Sally, for your wonderful book.

*Jane Di Paola*
*St. Katharine Drexel, Cape Coral, Florida*

In the early years of my priesthood I often wondered why Catholics left the Church. Was there something wrong with the Church? Something wrong with them? What were the real reasons?

As a Redemptorist missionary those questions bothered me. Then one night I was at a social function in St. Louis, Missouri. A man came up to me with a drink in his hand and said quite loudly: "Hey, Padre, I used to be a Catholic."

I said: "How long has it been?"

He said: "Twenty years."

I said: "Have you ever thought about coming back?"

He said: "Many times."

I said: "Why didn't you come back?"

He said: "Because no one ever asked me."

I asked him. He set down his drink and we talked. We talked for several days after that.

He and his family came back.

Then I wondered what would happen if we asked the sixteen million Catholics in this country to come back. I didn't know.

I was on the road for eighteen years with inactives and have spent the past four years on the Internet. On the road I met with about ten thousand. On the Internet, six thousand and more visit me every year.

When I left the road, a young, vibrant, and apostolic laywoman appeared, as if sent by God. Her name is Sally Mews and she has been working with the inactives for many years. She herself was out of the Church for a period of time. She can speak to the inactives better than I from her own pain-filled experiences.

Sally, married, one son, has a full-time job as the tax expert for a very large corporation. She spends her weekends on the road, with her husband, going from one diocese to another, setting up Catholics Returning Home, a program which she developed. It has proven to be an effective method of bringing many inactive Catholics back to the Church.

*†William F. McKee, C.Ss.R. (1920-2009)*
*St. Louis, Missouri*

## About Leonine Publishers

Leonine Publishers LLC makes fine Catholic literature available to Catholics throughout the English-speaking world. Leonine Publishers offers an innovative "hybrid" approach to book publication that helps authors as well as readers. Please visit our web site at www.leonine-publishers.com to learn more about us. Browse our online bookstore to find more solid Catholic titles to uplift, challenge, and inspire.

Our patron and namesake is Pope Leo XIII, a prudent, yet uncompromising pope during the stormy years at the close of the 19th century. Please join us as we ask his intercession for our family of readers and authors.

Do you have a book inside you? Visit our web site today. Leonine Publishers accepts manuscripts from Catholic authors like you. If your book is selected for publication, you will have an active part in the production process. This book is an example of our growing selection of literature for the busy Catholic reader of the 21st century.

www.leoninepublishers.com